"This is theology that is saturated with Sc[...] [...]the gospel, and earnestly intended for God's p[...] [...] This is theology *for* discipleship, and it is truly theology *as* discipleship. I learned much from reading it, and I was edified and challenged by it. It is a gift to us all."

Thomas H. McCall, Trinity Evangelical Divinity School

"This book is the prescription for all Christians who doubt theology's relevance for Christian living—and for all Christians who wonder what theology is about and how it works. Keith Johnson has 'nailed it' with this fine introductory work on the practical relevance of theology for Christian discipleship. Readers with an appreciation for theology will benefit from reading it as well. The chapters on Scripture express an enlightened evangelical approach to the Bible as the living Word of God."

Roger E. Olson, Foy Valentine Professor of Christian Theology and Ethics, George W. Truett Theological Seminary, Baylor University, Waco, Texas

"In *Theology as Discipleship*, Keith Johnson invites readers to inhabit a rich theological landscape as followers of Christ. Johnson's book overflows with wisdom and joy as he shows how Christians of all vocations are called to live in union with Christ, being reshaped by God's Word through the Spirit. This refreshing book is a wonderful theological companion for disciples of Jesus Christ."

J. Todd Billings, Gordon H. Girod Research Professor of Reformed Theology, Western Theological Seminary, Holland, Michigan

"Keith Johnson rightly understands that the practices of theology and discipleship are woven together; here he offers wise reflections on how to go about the task under the Word and Spirit and for the sake of the other. He ably points us in the right direction."

Kelly M. Kapic, author of *A Little Book for New Theologians*

"Keith Johnson has done a great service not only for the academic study of theology but for the church. In a time when the church's proclamation of its faith and the academy's reflection upon faith seem to be deeply divided, Johnson builds a bridge across the chasm. He shows not only why theology is necessary for the church but also why it can only find its true meaning when joined to the church's life as a form of Christian discipleship. Drawing upon the riches of the church's past yet grounded solidly in Scripture, this book expounds and reflects upon the gospel as the mystery of God's will that was foreordained in Christ and does so in a way that is not only deeply learned and careful, but also caring and clear. For those wondering why they should bother with theology at all, they will find here a wise and compassionate answer. For those who turn theology into a practice of intellectual theatrics or point of pride, they will find here an incisive and needed corrective. This book is, in short, a wonderful and exemplary primer to the task of theology that deserves many readers."

Kimlyn J. Bender, George W. Truett Theological Seminary, Baylor University

THEOLOGY AS

DISCIPLESHIP

KEITH L. JOHNSON

IVP Academic

An imprint of InterVarsity Press
Downers Grove, Illinois

InterVarsity Press
P.O. Box 1400, Downers Grove, IL 60515-1426
ivpress.com
email@ivpress.com

InterVarsity Press® is the book-publishing division of InterVarsity Christian Fellowship/USA®, a movement of
students and faculty active on campus at hundreds of universities, colleges and schools of nursing in the United
States of America, and a member movement of the International Fellowship of Evangelical Students. For
information about local and regional activities, visit intervarsity.org.

Scripture quotations, unless otherwise noted, are from the New Revised Standard Version of the Bible, copyright
1989 by the Division of Christian Education of the National Council of the Churches of Christ in the USA. Used by
permission. All rights reserved.

While any stories in this book are true, some names and identifying information may have been changed to protect
the privacy of individuals.

Cover design: Cindy Kiple
Interior design: Beth McGill
Images: Washing Feet by Laura James/Laura James Fine Arts, laurajamesart.com

ISBN 978-0-8308-4034-2 (print)
ISBN 978-0-8308-8017-1 (digital)

Printed in the United States of America ∞

Library of Congress Cataloging-in-Publication Data

Johnson, Keith L.
  Theology as discipleship / Keith L. Johnson.
    pages cm
  Includes index.
  ISBN 978-0-8308-4034-2 (pbk. : alk. paper)
  1. Theology, Practical. 2. Christian life. I. Title.
  BV4.J64 2015
  230—dc23

                                                                                    2015033926

P 23 22 21 20 19 18 17 16 15 14 13 12 11 10 9 8 7 6 5 4 3 2 1
Y 34 33 32 31 30 29 28 27 26 25 24 23 22 21 20 19 18 17 16 15

For my students

CONTENTS

CONTENTS

ACKNOWLEDGMENTS

∅

This book was written in conversation with my students at Wheaton College, particularly those who have participated in my introductory courses. The opportunity to teach them theology has been one of God's great gifts to me, because the challenge of doing so has propelled me further on the path of discipleship. This book is dedicated to them.

I particularly want to acknowledge a few students whose questions and insights have prompted certain lines of thought in this book. The importance of figuring out the place of academic theology in the life of faith became clear to me during conversations with the students from the Wheaton in the Holy Lands program in the summer of 2009. Those long hours of discussion and debate on the bus or over coffee form the background of many of these chapters. I especially want to acknowledge the contributions of Abby Anderson, Hannah Buchanan, Rebekah Pahl, Graham Smith, Annika Turner, Garret Zajac and Emily Zeller. Other students who inspired sections of this book include Sarah Kennedy, who put into words many of the worries students have about academic theology; Michael Rau and Anna Jacobson, who relentlessly probed me with questions during my office hours about how theology can be done faithfully; Meredith Hawkins, whose integrity and humility showed me what a faithful theological student looks like; and Libby Boehne, who lives out much of what I describe in these pages in her life and ministry. To all of these students—and to so many others who remain unnamed here but are known to me—I express my deep appreciation.

It is hard to imagine managing my daily life without the help of my teaching assistants and researchers, including Kathryn Heidelberger and Genny Austin, who helped me find the time and space to work on this book. I am also grateful to some outstanding students who offered early feedback on this manuscript, including Stephen Ticsay, Anna Jacobson and Sarah Johnson. Sarah in particular made some very helpful editorial suggestions. The idea for this project arose as the result of conversations with my colleague Beth Felker Jones about the relationship between Christian doctrine and practice. She is one of many wonderful scholars and teachers I work with in the Biblical and Theological Studies Department at Wheaton College. I particularly want to note my colleagues with offices located on my hallway: George Kalantzis, David Lauber, Vince Bacote and Gregory Lee. We are united by a love for our students and a desire to serve Christ and his church, and they make coming to work each day a lot of fun. Greg also is to be noted for his particularly helpful suggestions on this manuscript. I also am grateful for the support and encouragement of several wonderful administrators, including Jeffrey Bingham, Jill Baumgaertner, Stanton Jones and Philip Ryken.

My friends have been a constant source of encouragement. In this regard, I make special mention of Kevin Hector, Myles Werntz, Wesley Keyes, Kevin Roberts, Sean Allen, Chris Thacker, Erin Conaway, Matt Cook, Josh Haynes, Matt Sciba and Britt Young. I also have benefited from the support of the editors of InterVarsity Press, including Brannon Ellis and David Congdon. David in particular offered helpful insights throughout the process and saved me from more than one mistake.

Finally, I am grateful for the love of Julie, Everett and Blake. The fact that God has granted me the chance to live life with them shows that he is a God of grace beyond all measure. I also am thankful for the constant companionship of my dog Jasper, who slept near my desk as I wrote much of this manuscript.

PREFACE

T his book emerges out of my experience teaching theology to under-
graduates. Although my students typically enjoy learning the material, they often have difficulty relating it to their Christian lives. The
question appears like clockwork in nearly every course. *What difference
does theology actually make for our lives?* Often it appears during our
discussion of the doctrine of the Trinity, or perhaps while we are looking
at the distinctions that prompted the divisions of the Reformation. The
arguments of previous centuries seem archaic and irrelevant to the faith
of my students. *Why does this matter?* Convictions that prompted heated
debates and church divisions in the past seem unimportant today.
Shouldn't we just focus on following Jesus? And my students are not the
only ones with these sorts of questions. I have found over the years that
many if not most Christians who study theology either have these same
questions or have had them at some point. I often ask them myself.

The fact that these kind of questions can be asked at all—and, more
importantly, the fact they are asked for sincere and substantive reasons—
reveals a problem in the way we teach and learn theology. It demonstrates,
for example, that the discipline of theology has become so divorced from
the everyday practices of the Christian life that it is difficult for smart and
committed Christians to figure out how they relate. It also reveals that the
long-acknowledged tension between the academic discipline of theology
and the life of discipleship to Jesus Christ may, in fact, be a great chasm.

It is possible for a Christian to participate in the church for years and never engage in disciplined theological thinking about core Christian doctrines or the history of the church's debates about them. It also is possible for academic theologians to devote their careers to the discipline and never be asked to translate or apply the content of their scholarship to the concrete realities that shape the daily life of the church. Taken together, these problems point to another, even deeper issue: we often pursue theological learning without a clear understanding of how and why we do so.

These problems form the background to this book. In the pages that follow, I argue that the discipline of theology and a life of discipleship to Jesus Christ are integrally related because the practice of theology is one of the ways we participate in the life of the triune God. I make this case by explaining what theology is, how theology is possible and what it looks like for a theologian to practice the discipline as an act of faith and obedience. My goal is to show how the study of theology enriches Christian practice and how faithful obedience to Christ enables the learning of theology.

Two commitments guide my approach along the way. First, because this book arises out of my introductory courses in theology, I have written it with this context in mind. My hope is that this volume might find a place in similar courses at colleges and seminaries alongside the main textbook and primary texts. I also hope it will be enriching not only to scholars but also to pastors and laypeople who engage in theological study. With these audiences in view, I have tried to write so that the argument will be accessible to beginners but not simplistic to the advanced. I have minimized the use of technical terms, avoided scholarly rabbit trails and tried to interact with major theologians and texts likely to be discussed in an introductory theology course. At the same time, I have tried to make a substantive contribution to the discipline. This dual audience means that beginners at times may feel like they are swimming in deeper waters than they had planned, while the more advanced reader may wonder why I have not taken certain paths. I ask for the reader's patience or charity if and when these situations arise.

Second, the argument proceeds under the conviction that theological

claims should be offered together with the biblical exegesis that supports
and shapes them. Theology is not identical to biblical exegesis. In fact, as
will become clear, theologians often must go beyond the letter of Scripture
precisely in order to be faithful to it. Yet the aims of our theological work
cannot be other than, or independent of, the aims toward which Scripture
itself moves. Among other things, Scripture enables us to see the true
nature of created reality and history, and one of our key tasks is to figure
out how to participate in reality rightly by finding our place in the history
narrated by the text. For these reasons, much of the argument presented
here takes place through close theological readings of Scripture. The goal
is to lay out these readings as the framework from which we can begin
to understand where and how theologians fit into what God is doing in
history through the saving work of Jesus Christ and the Holy Spirit.

The argument proceeds over the course of seven chapters. Chapter one
explains the place of theology in the Christian life and offers an account
of why some Christians believe the discipline of theology inhibits rather
than enriches our discipleship to Christ. The origin of these worries is
explained by way of a historical account of the shifting practice of theology over the centuries. This account will show that the discipline of
theology has a dual accountability to both the church and the academy
and that theologians have not always navigated this dual relationship
very well. The chapter concludes with a description of the goal of the
book: to rebuild our understanding of how and why the discipline of
theology operates so that we might overcome some of the legitimate
worries Christians have about it.

Chapter two begins this rebuilding process by arguing that the whole
of created reality and history is ordered by the person and work of Jesus
Christ. The argument begins where theology itself begins: with our confession of faith that Jesus Christ is Lord and our belief that God raised
him from the dead. On the basis of this confession, we describe our place
in God's eternal plan for reality and history. We then explain what it
means for believers to be united to Jesus Christ by the power of his Holy
Spirit as well as the implications of this union for our knowledge of God
and creation.

Chapter three describes what it looks like for a believer to live in union with Jesus Christ in the power of his Spirit within the context of God's eternal plan. This description centers on God's intention that his people live in partnership with him as he works out his divine will for created history. We figure out the shape of this partnership by finding our place in the biblical narrative. The chapter explores our creation in God's image and likeness, the consequences of our fall into sin and the pattern of salvation history as demonstrated in God's relationship with the people of Israel and the life of Israel's Messiah, Jesus of Nazareth. The implications of our partnership with Christ for our relationship with God and others in the church are then explored. The chapter concludes with an examination of the effect this partnership has for the practice of theology by describing how Christ determines our application of words to God.

Chapter four explores God's relationship to the text of the Bible. After accounting for the way God relates to and uses human words within the context of his eternal plan, we describe the doctrine of the inspiration of Scripture through the lens of an exegetical test case: the apostle John's description of Jesus' debate with the Pharisees about his relationship to God's promises to Abraham (Jn 8). Our close reading of this passage puts us in position to argue that we read and interpret Scripture rightly when we do so in community with Jesus Christ himself.

Chapter five builds on this argument by describing what this kind of interpretation looks like. In conversation with Augustine's argument that our reading of Scripture should be measured by how it relates to our love of God and neighbor, we examine the Spirit's work to illumine Scripture through our own internal transformation and our external relationships to other believers. Again, this argument is developed by way of a test case, this time looking at the debates surrounding Gentile circumcision involving Paul and other apostles in the early church. The chapter ends with an account of the relationship between our reading of Scripture and the practice of theology.

Chapter six describes the practice of theology in terms of our participation in the mind of Jesus Christ. The description begins with an exploration of Paul's account of the "mind of Christ" in Philippians 2 and 1

Corinthians 2. Our participation in the mind of Christ is made concrete through an examination of how Christ displays the content of his mind through his actions of humility and obedience. The chapter concludes with an account of theological method that corresponds to our life of discipleship to Jesus.

Chapter seven builds upon the argument of the prior chapters by offering nine characteristics that theologians will display as they practice the discipline of theology within the context of their participation in the life of God through Christ and the Spirit. Together, these characteristics show how the practice of theology corresponds to, rather than conflicts with, a life of discipleship to Jesus Christ.

My hope for the readers of this book is that they will see more clearly how their study of theology fits with and corresponds to the rest of their Christian life. One of the key tasks of a disciple is to seek to understand everything—from the nature of God's eternal being to the entire created order to our own lives—in the light of Jesus, because he is the one "in whom are hidden all the treasures of wisdom and knowledge" (Col 2:3). While organized theological study is not the only way we can seek this kind of understanding, it can and does make substantive contributions to this process. Among other things, it helps us develop our intellectual skills, exposes us to new and enriching ideas and gives us access to the collected wisdom of the church throughout the centuries. Seen in this light, the chance to practice the discipline of theology comes to us a gift from God, one that can help us have minds and bodies that are "worthy of the gospel of Christ" (Phil 1:27). My prayer for this book is that it will help us receive and then use this great gift to the glory of God.

one

RECOVERING THEOLOGY

⌀

The word *theology* comes from the Greek terms *logos*, often translated as "reason" or "word," and *theos*, which means "God." We practice theology whenever we think or speak about God. We are doing theology when we pray, worship, read Scripture, teach others about the faith and make decisions about how to live in a right relationship to God. In this sense, every Christian practices theology every day.

To illustrate, consider the claim "God is good." We can imagine using this claim in a wide variety of contexts. It could be turned into a declaration and applied to God during prayer or worship as a form of praise. We might run across it while reading Scripture and use it to inform our understanding of God's being and character. It could be offered as an explanation for why God acted in a particular way in the past, or it might be employed as an argument for why we should act in a certain way in the present. The list of possible uses could go on. Every one of these uses requires that we practice theology. After all, who is this "God" we are talking about? The word *God* does not sit as an empty concept in our minds. It has a meaning that has been acquired over the course of our lives, some of it by way of our personal experience with God and some through the instruction of others. This meaning is working in the background whenever we say the word *God*. The same thing is happening with our use of "good." We use this word all the time, such as when we say, "The weather is good," or "He is a good person." This everyday usage forms the background of our use of this word to describe God. This makes things complicated. We might say, "Good dog!" to our puppy, and then say "God is good" a few minutes later. Certainly, we do not mean exactly the same thing by the word *good* in both sentences. What is the difference between our use of the word *good* when we apply it to God as opposed to our puppy? The task of answering this question—even implicitly and instinctively—requires the practice of theology.

This illustration shows, however, that even if a Christian has never engaged in formal theological study, he or she already operates with a functional theology at every moment of his or her life. Our functional theology consists of our default assumptions about who God is, what God is like and how God relates to us.[1] These assumptions work in the background of all our thinking and speaking about God. They affect every claim we make about God because we filter every word we apply to God through them. So, when we read in the Psalms that "God is good" (Ps 73:1), our functional theology determines how we understand the meaning of the words in this sentence. In fact, we have never read or interpreted any word of Scripture apart from this kind of preunderstanding. Such is the case for every other claim we have heard or said about God. Theology has been a part of our lives at every moment.

The problem is that our functional theology can be wrong. God is good, but his goodness is not the same as that of the weather, a person or a puppy. Figuring out the nature of the similarities and differences between God's goodness and these creaturely examples of goodness can be difficult. In our everyday life, for instance, we might think that a good person would not permit innocent people to suffer if he could prevent it. On this basis, we might say that, because God is good, he also would never allow the innocent to suffer unjustly. Yet this is precisely what God does: he sometimes permits the innocent to suffer, as he did in the case of Jesus Christ and believers in the early church (2 Thess 1:4-5). It can be challenging to figure out why we say "God is good" even though he will-

---

[1]The term "functional theology" comes from J. Todd Billings, *The Word of God for the People of God: An Entryway into the Theological Interpretation of Scripture* (Grand Rapids: Eerdmans, 2010), 11-17.

ingly permits suffering, while a human who does the same thing normally would not be considered good. This challenge is so great, in fact, that sometimes people draw incorrect conclusions about God based on their assumptions about what he must be like: "A good God would never allow the innocent to suffer." Multiply this potential for error by every single word we use for God, and it becomes possible, if not likely, that we will apply words to God incorrectly by drawing mistaken conclusions based on our faulty assumptions of what God must be like. As a result, we often end up with an incorrect picture of God and say untrue things about him.

Our potential for error explains why we need the kind of formal theological instruction that makes up the discipline of theology. The discipline of theology is the name for the organized practice of theological reasoning that directs our thoughts and speech about God so that they correspond to who God is and what God is like. This discipline came into existence in response to the fact that our functional theology does not always match the reality of God. Its goal is to shape our ideas and words about God so that that our functional theology corresponds to the truth about his divine being and character. As a discipline, theology developed over the centuries as prominent thinkers and leaders in the church responded to theological problems and questions by offering guidelines for how to speak and think about God correctly. These guidelines were drawn from the church's reading of Scripture and took form in the church's creeds, which serve as summary statements of right thinking and speaking about core matters of the Christian faith. The church considers thinking and speech about God to be orthodox when it corresponds to this creedal tradition and heretical when it does not.

In the present, the discipline of theology takes place as theologians write books, articles and biblical commentaries offering insights about how to think and speak about God correctly. They teach others by instructing them about errors the church has fallen into in the past so that we do not repeat them in the present. They also offer practical guidance for addressing the challenging questions Christians face today, such as those prompted by the existence of suffering, cultural changes brought about by new technology and the complicated interaction between adherents of different religions that shapes the modern world.

CONCERNS WITH THEOLOGY

Given its noble purpose, its prominent place in church history and the real contributions it makes to the church's contemporary life, one would think that the discipline of theology has a positive reputation among Christians—but it does not. Every Christian has a functional theology, but not every Christian has a positive view of the discipline of theology. In fact, many smart and faithful Christians cringe when they hear the word *theology* due to the negative connotations the discipline carries. Some even reject the very idea of theology and insist that they can live faithfully without it simply by trusting God and believing the words of Scripture. There are at least three reasons why this negative view of theology has developed over time.

First, many Christians believe that the formal study of theology distracts us from the most important activities of the Christian life. Every Christian wants to think and speak about God correctly. But does the formal and organized study of theology help or hinder us in doing so? This is a matter of debate. Even though much sincere effort has been put into the discipline of theology over the centuries, many Christians believe it brings few benefits and many dangers for the church as a whole. Most of us know people who live faithful lives even though they have never formally studied theology; and at the same time, many of us also know or have heard about people who know a lot of theology but live hypocritically or without faith. Such examples prompt the warnings many students receive about theology professors who lead students astray or students who have lost their faith as a result of advanced theological study.

Behind many of these warnings is the worry that the discipline of theology unnecessarily complicates the faith by making it more complex and confusing than it needs to be. Paul warned that we should "avoid stupid controversies" about doctrinal matters because they are "unprofitable and worthless" (Tit 3:9). Instead of spending time and energy debating complex details, shouldn't we focus on the central and most clearly understood commandments of the Christian life, such as the task of loving God and neighbor (Lk 10:27)? After all, if one can live faithfully without theological study—and if such study sometimes leads believers down the wrong path by unnecessarily complicating the faith—then it makes sense to invest our time and resources elsewhere. Doesn't the discipline of theology distract us from the real work of the church, such as praying, worshiping, sharing the gospel and serving others?

Second, many Christians believe the study of theology inhibits rather than helps our discipleship to Jesus. One way it does so is by undermining our confidence in the content of the Christian faith. Because the process of engaging new material inevitably challenges long-held assumptions, exposes faulty patterns of thinking and prompts new and difficult questions, beginning students of theology often find themselves intellectually shaken by their study. Even though their new theological insights may help students begin to think and speak about God better than they could before, the process also often leaves them feeling ignorant. "How could I have been a Christian my whole life and not have known any of this before?" Instead of becoming stronger in the faith and better equipped to work and serve within the church, the new theologian often is embarrassed by all that he or she does not know and paralyzed by the prospect of looking foolish when he or she speaks. Theology in this case operates more like law than grace, and the theologian retreats from doing anything at all lest his or her ignorance be displayed for all to see. The result, as Helmut Thielicke puts it, is that a "lively young Christian is horribly squeezed to death in the formal armor of abstract ideas."[2] Theological study that should be freeing and enriching instead becomes restrictive and debilitating.

The mirror image of this problem is that theological study sometimes leaves people overconfident in their abilities. At some point, nearly everyone has been in a Bible study or church meeting with someone who not only thinks he or she has all the right answers but who also seems

---

[2]Helmut Thielicke, *A Little Exercise for Young Theologians* (Grand Rapids: Eerdmans, 1962), 8.

intent on showing that everyone else's answers are wrong. Paul warns about these tendencies when he says that "knowledge puffs up" (1 Cor 8:1). Some people, he tells Timothy, have "a morbid craving for controversy and for disputes about words," which causes "envy, dissension, slander, base suspicions, and wrangling" within the church (1 Tim 6:4-5). They seem to enjoy arguing with their fellow Christians about doctrinal matters, because doing so gives them a sense of purpose and identity. This identity often involves a sense of entitlement and elitism, as if their learning places them above the unenlightened masses who make up the large part of the church. Worse still, theologians sometimes use their skills to manipulate the content of the faith so that it conforms to their own ideas and goals. Paul talks about this tendency when he said that some people's "itching ears" lead them "to accumulate for themselves teachers to suit their own desires." Their theological learning leaves them worse off than before, because it enables them to "turn away from listening to the truth and wander away to myths" they have devised for themselves (2 Tim 4:3-4).

Third, many people think the formal study of theology produces unnecessary divisions in the church. Even though reading the texts of the great theologians can bring great benefits, it also can produce a sense of disillusionment. Many of the theologians widely considered to be among the best thinkers in church history starkly disagree with one another about core matters of doctrine. Not all of them can be right, and in fact, many of them think the others are gravely wrong. Often, these great theologians have entire schools of thought centered around their views which stand in opposition to other schools of thought based on the work of other theologians. The existence of these divergent schools of thought puts us in a situation where the label "Christian" is not enough. We also have to figure out which *kind* of Christian we are—whether it is Thomist, Lutheran, Calvinist, Arminian, or so on. While such labels can help us recognize important differences between various approaches to theology, they also can divide Christians from one another and hurt the church's witness.

Paul makes this point when he criticizes the Corinthians for engaging in "jealousy and quarreling" between those who held to the teachings of Apollos and those who identified with Paul himself. Instead of starting with their immature "human inclinations," Paul says, the Corinthians should view all their various teachers as "God's servants, working together" for a "common purpose" (1 Cor 3:2-9). Paul's point is clear: our theological distinctions are not irrelevant, but even so, they must be relativized by our common bond in Christ and commitment to the church's mission. Any theological distinction that unnecessarily causes us to lose sight of this unity and purpose undermines the integrity of the church and the gospel it proclaims. The problem, as many Christians point out, is that Paul's instructions have rarely been followed by the church's theologians. In fact, more often than not, theological debates proceed just like contemporary political debates, with each side defending its views at all costs while assuming that their opponents are not only wrong but also morally and intellectually deficient in some way. This leads to a type of theological partisanship, where adherents of a certain view repeat their party line without charitably considering other arguments or striving for reconciliation with their opponents. In this case, the goal of theological study becomes less about knowing God or enriching the church than about building up one's side and bringing down one's enemies.

Such activities prompt some Christians to conclude that the study of theology, while noble in and of itself, almost inevitably become a means by which the theologian serves his or her own interests. James makes this point when he says that conflicts and disputes often stem from our desire of things we want but do not have (Jas 4:1-2). Just like the disciples argued among themselves about "which one of them was the greatest" (Lk 9:46), Christians often seek a position of authority over their fellow Christians. Theology often is employed as a tool to achieve this goal. If a theologian can prove that his or her opponents are wrong about important matters of doctrine, then he or she can justify having a position of influence and power over them. Paul encountered this problem when he was challenged by teachers in Philippi who worked against him out of "envy and rivalry" in line with their own "selfish ambition" (Phil 1:15-17). Then as today, such an approach hurts the church, because as James notes, "where there is envy and selfish ambition, there will also be disorder and wickedness of every kind" (Jas 3:16).

These are the sorts of consequences that prompt faithful Christians to have a negative view of theology. If theological learning can and often does produce unnecessary and sinful divisions in the church—and if these divisions are often about the desire of some to gain positions of power and influence over others for their own benefit—then does the discipline of theology truly benefit the church?

WHAT WENT WRONG?

One explanation for why and how the formal practice of theology became suspect in the eyes of many Christians involves the shifting occupations of theologians.[3] For much of Christian history, theology was practiced almost exclusively from within the church. Most early theologians, for example, were bishops and priests responsible for leading the church in its worship, teaching and ministry. Their formal theological study often stemmed from their desire to help their congregants avoid errors, understand Scripture and grow in their devotion to God. Even when they argued against other theologians, they did so not for themselves but for the sake of the church's members. For example, the theological orations of Gregory Nazianzus against the Eunomian heresy were delivered as sermons to help his congregation "avoid being swept way" by this false teaching.[4] Likewise, Cyril of Alexandria composed public letters to Nestorius not only to challenge Nestorius's questionable claims about Jesus but also to inform other church leaders about his errors so they could instruct their congregations about Christological matters.[5] In these sorts of ways, the bishops and priests used the discipline of theology to further their pastoral

---

[3]For this insight, see Jaroslav Pelikan, *The Christian Tradition: A History of the Development of Doctrine, 1: The Emergence of the Catholic Tradition (100–600)* (Chicago: University of Chicago Press, 1975), 5.

[4]Gregory Nazianzus, Oration 30.1, from *On God and Christ: The Five Theological Orations and Two Letters to Cledonius*, trans. Fredrick Williams and Lionel Wickham (Crestwood, NY: St. Vladimir's Seminary Press, 2002), 93.

[5]See John McGuckin, *Saint Cyril of Alexandria and the Christological Controversy* (Crestwood, NY: St. Vladimir's Seminary Press, 2004).

aims and to promote the doctrinal integrity of the church as a whole.

The same could be said of the theologians who lived and worked from within the monasteries. Although they were never totally separated from the life and work of the institutional church, the distinct rhythms of the monastic life often led these monks to bring their theological insights together with spiritual practices related to purification of the mind and body. Their isolation also gave them the time to think carefully about difficult theological topics such as God's triune being or the nature of God's relationship to created life. This work supplemented the theology of the bishops and priests in important ways. Augustine's conversion stands as a case in point. Even though he greatly admired his bishop Ambrose, Augustine recalls that Ambrose did not know about Augustine's "spiritual turmoil" because he was too busy meeting the needs of his congregation. "The crowds of people who came to him on business impeded me," he recalls, "allowing me little opportunity either to talk or to listen to him."[6] A turning point came when Augustine read *The Life of Antony*, a book describing the famous monk's spiritual life and practices. Antony's example challenged Augustine's view of the world and prompted a line of thinking that eventually led to his conversion.[7] This influence lingered even after Augustine became a bishop, as the monastic style of theology and the example of monks like Antony continued to shape his writings and ministry.

A common factor uniting the work of the bishops, priests and monks was their assumption that theological study should be integrally related to a life of discipleship. Persons who wanted to study theology needed to "purify themselves" in the pattern of Christ (1 Jn 3:3). This meant that formal theological study was not something that just anyone could do. For instance, Gregory Nazianzus argues that theology should be pursued only by "those who have been tested and have found a sound footing in study, and more importantly, have undergone, or at the very least are

---

[6]Augustine, *The Confessions* 6.3.3, trans. Maria Boulding, O.S.B. (Hyde Park, NY: New City Press, 1997), 99.

[7]Augustine, *The Confessions* 8.15; 8.29 (trans. Boulding), 157, 168.

undergoing, purification of body and soul."[8] If the mind and body are integrally related to one another, then the theological formation of the mind must go hand in hand with acts of bodily obedience in the pattern of Christ. "Do we commend hospitality?" Gregory asks. "Do we admire brotherly love, wifely affection, virginity, feeding the poor, singing psalms, night-long vigils, penitence? Do we mortify the body with fasting? Do we, through prayer, take up our abode with God? . . . Do we establish our mastery over our passions, mindful of the nobility of our second birth?" Gregory insists that the answer to all these questions must be yes, because such actions work to "smooth the theologian in us, like a statue, into beauty."[9] Theological learning is pursued rightly when it occurs within the context of a life of discipleship, because the practices of discipleship enable and enrich our pursuit of theological knowledge.

This presupposed connection between theology and discipleship slowly began to change during the medieval period when the discipline of theology became part of the curriculum of the university. Theologians began to pursue their work primarily from the role of professor, and this shift carried several benefits. The university provided theologians a space akin to the monastery, freeing them from administrative burdens and giving them the chance to study and write for extended periods. At the same time, theologians were able to remain more connected to the institutional church than the monks had been, because they could participate in local church services and live in direct contact with the church's members and leaders. Their teaching duties also put them into conversation with a wide variety of people from across the culture, including scholars from other academic disciplines. Now more than ever, theologians had the opportunity to learn from external sources and incorporate new ways of thinking into their doctrinal work. Theologians became portals through which the church received an influx of fresh ideas and insights that enriched its internal thinking and practice. This presented theologians with exciting opportunities. From their vantage point in the university, theologians could draw connections between the church's

---

[8]Gregory Nazianzus, Oration 27.3, from *On God and Christ*, 27.
[9]Gregory Nazianzus, Oration 27.7, from *On God and Christ*, 30.

theology, the practical lives of everyday believers and the questions central to the culture at large. These new connections became the starting point from which they were able to make innovative and lasting contributions to the church to help it pursue its mission in the world.

This ideal was challenged, however, as the universities changed from their medieval to their modern form. These shifts stemmed from changes in the way the universities determined what counted as true academic learning. As Nicholas Wolterstorff explains, a university's standard of scholarship, teaching and learning tends to be drawn from disciplines that are considered "paradigmatic" within the wider culture.[10] In medieval universities, this position had been held by theology, which had been regarded as the most noble discipline and the one by which the others were measured.[11] By the time of the Enlightenment, however, the natural and social sciences began to replace theology in this central role. These disciplines brought with them a slate of new assumptions about the nature of God and his relationship with creation. For example, many scientists at the time were influenced by Deism, which meant they believed that God had created the world and then left it to operate according to its own natural laws. On this basis, they assumed that the content of God's wisdom is embedded in, and can be known from, the structure of the universe itself. They also held that because humans have rational minds that reflect God's own image, every human must be naturally capable of discovering the truth about God simply by acquiring an understanding of the natural order of the universe and then conforming his or her thinking to it.[12]

These new assumptions changed what counted as proper learning

---

[10]Nicholas Wolterstorff, "The Travail of Theology in the Modern Academy," in *The Future of Theology: Essays in Honor of Jürgen Moltmann*, ed. Miroslav Volf, Carmen Kreig and Thomas Kucharz (Grand Rapids: Eerdmans, 1996), 39. Also see John Webster, "Theological Theology," in *Confessing God: Essays in Christian Dogmatics II* (London: T&T Clark, 2005), 13-17. My analysis of theology's place in the modern university is indebted to the arguments presented in these two essays.

[11]See, for example, the remarks of Thomas Aquinas in *Summa Theologica* I, q. 1, a. 5. All quotations from the *Summa Theologica* in this volume are drawn from *Basic Writings of Saint Thomas Aquinas*, ed. Anton C. Pegis, 2 vols. (New York: Random House, 1945).

[12]On this point, see Charles Taylor, *Sources of the Self: The Making of Modern Identity* (Cambridge, MA: Harvard University Press, 1989), 271-74.

within the university. No longer did scholars assume that they must turn to Scripture or the church to know the truth about God; instead, they needed to turn to the order of nature and then observe its processes rationally and objectively.[13] They argued that we see things rationally and objectively when we are free of biases that distort our ability to sort through the evidence we encounter. A discipline is truly "scientific" when it can account for the way it filters out any biases present within it so that the scholar can observe and assess her subject matter in an objective way. Biases enter into our thinking in two key ways. First, we become biased when we assume that our approach is the only way something can be done rather than merely one approach that reflects our own particular time, place or culture. For example, even though we may have strong convictions about certain ethical or moral matters, these sorts of convictions differ widely between cultures and periods of history. If we are to approach ethical issues scientifically, we must set aside our personal commitments and proceed according to universal maxims applicable to every person in all times and places. While we are free to maintain our personal views in our private life, only those commitments that are universally applicable should shape our academic research and its conclusions. Second, biases also tend to come from a misplaced reliance on sources of authority. To proceed scientifically, we cannot assume that any particular source inherently carries authority such that it can be trusted without question. Rather, we must evaluate every so-called authoritative source in order to determine what, if anything, within this source corresponds to the objective standard of critical reason. Only claims that correspond to this standard can be used as the basis for knowledge.[14]

As theologians faced these new criteria for their academic work within the university, they found themselves pulled in two different directions. On the one hand, they still had the task of contributing to the doctrinal and spiritual life of the church. Because the church operated from the

---

[13]See Michael Allen Gillespie, *The Theological Origins of Modernity* (Chicago: University of Chicago Press, 2008), 16-17.

[14]For an exploration of this point, see Jeffrey Stout, *The Flight from Authority: Religion, Morality and the Quest for Autonomy* (Notre Dame, IN: University of Notre Dame Press, 1981), 149-50.

starting point of faith, assumed the accuracy of authoritative sources like the Bible and believed that right thinking must go together with particular moral actions, many theologians within the university still sought to explain the contribution of theology in these terms. On the other hand, theologians felt pressure to justify their conclusions according to the academic criteria that governed the university. This meant that rather than starting with faith—which might distort their ability to assess evidence rationally—they had to begin with universally accepted premises and employ the methods of critical reason. No longer could they appeal to the authority of the Bible or the church's tradition to defend their claims. Instead, they had to determine which claims from these sources could be objectively verified as a reliable guide to rational thinking for every human being.

To deal with this tension, many theologians tried to mediate between the church and the university by performing theological work that both contributed to the church and met the standards of the academy. One of the most impressive attempts of this sort was put forth by Friedrich Schleiermacher, a pastor and theologian in Berlin at the beginning of the nineteenth century. He begins with the premise that the discipline of theology must include both "scientific information and practical instruction" and that each element must be maintained in its full integrity.[15] He insists that any academic study of theology that has no relation to the church's practical life "ceases to be theological." At the same time, he argues that a church that fails to explain its beliefs and practices according to the standards of critical reason undermines its own "historical importance" by exercising "a mere muddle of attempted influence" in society.[16] The way forward is for church leaders to become academics who help the church adhere to the standards of critical reason while also showing those outside the church that anyone thinking rationally should turn to the church to find reason in its highest form.

To this end, Schleiermacher argues that academic theologians should

---

[15]Friedrich Schleiermacher, *Brief Outline of Theology as a Field of Study*, 3rd ed., ed. and trans. Terrence N. Tice (Louisville, KY: Westminster John Knox, 2011), 3 (paragraph 5).
[16]Ibid., 6, 2, 7 (paragraphs 6, 2 and 12).

engage in two central tasks. First, they should demonstrate that the church's practices are "a necessary element for the development of the human spirit" rather than the product of their own specific commitments.[17] To do this, theologians have to assess the church's practices with "complete impartiality" according to the standards of critical reason and then show how these practices relate to every person no matter his or her specific cultural or religious background.[18] Second, they should employ a "genuinely deliberative character" as they direct the church's thought, worship and ministry.[19] Their goal will be to refine the church's beliefs and practices by exposing its untested presuppositions, critically assessing authoritative sources like the Bible and aligning its doctrine and activities with the universal standards of critical reason. Although this process of refinement may be difficult and painful, it ultimately will strengthen the church by transposing its traditional formulations into terms that can be accepted and understood by any rational person. This will enable the church to fulfill its mission more successfully, because now the church will be able to explain and defend its faith by the standards of rationality that govern society as a whole.

This twofold vision for relationship between theology and the church shaped the way Schleiermacher approached theological education. In his view, the primary goal of theological learning is to transform a student from a "mere carrier of tradition" into a thinker who is capable of engaging the best insights of the age from across every discipline.[20] Every theologian not only must be a saint, therefore, but a scholar as well. This means that theological training should occur primarily within the university and proceed in line with the standards of critical scholarship. Academic training would not lead theologians away from but into the church, because the university should have a vested interest in the church as the place where the highest ideals of human reason are fulfilled.

This vision for theological education was deeply influential and

---

[17]Ibid., 10-11 (paragraphs 21-22).
[18]Ibid., 71 (paragraph 193).
[19]Ibid., 97 (paragraph 259).
[20]Ibid., 9 (paragraphs 18-19).

widely adopted, even among those who disagreed with the content of Schleiermacher's theology. The result was a broad shift in the way Christians practiced the discipline. Whereas theologians once had been accountable strictly to the standards of the church and its mission, now they were accountable to the standards of both the church *and* the university. This dual accountability changed the way they interacted with non-theological disciplines. The best theologians had always engaged the insights of other disciplines, including the sciences. They always had done so, however, with the goal of drawing these disciplines into theology's intellectual framework—a framework built on the presuppositions that follow from the confession of faith in Jesus Christ. Now the direction of movement reversed. Theologians interacted with these same disciplines not in order to reframe them in light of their faith but to secure theology's place in the academy alongside every other discipline. The result was that, along with the need to establish their claims according to Scripture and the church's tradition, theologians now also felt pressure to justify their claims according to the academic criteria governing the university.

This pressure created several problems. The most critical problem was that the standards governing the university had been derived from disciplines which proceeded on the basis of presuppositions about the nature of reality and history that were markedly different from those that traditionally governed the practice of theology. As a result, as John Webster notes, theology now had to be practiced in "alienation from its own subject matter and procedures" if it was to remain legitimately academic.[21] Formerly, theologians had pursued theological training in order to acquire knowledge, habits and skills that would shape them into the pattern of Jesus Christ for the sake of their service to the church. Spiritual formation and active participation in the life and ministry of the church were a central part of theological training because these activities were thought to be intrinsic to the pursuit of the knowledge of God. Now, with the discipline of theology housed primarily in the university, the primary

---

[21]Webster, "Theological Theology," 17.

goal of theological education was to provide students with the technical skills they needed to perform responsible critical enquiry so that the church's faith and practice could be brought in line with the standards of critical reason.[22] The difference between the two approaches changed the way theologians operated. Rather than beginning from the presupposition that theology and discipleship are intrinsically related to one another, theologians proceeded as if the practices of the faith—such as worship, prayer and discipleship to Christ—existed in a realm distinct from the practice of theology. A life of discipleship and the assumptions, patterns of thinking and practices associated with it became just one, optional way a theologian might apply his or her theological training. But by no means was it assumed that the theologian needed to make this kind of application in order to practice the discipline rightly.

This historical shift and the methodological changes it produced help explain the tensions that exist between the discipline of theology and many Christians. Despite their great learning, theologians have sometimes struggled to apply their insights to the life of the church, or even to their own spiritual lives, because they have not been trained or required to do so. An academic theologian can practice the discipline within the university and never need to connect his or her theology to the everyday practices of the church. Some theologians even hold themselves at arm's length from the church by adopting an attitude of detachment toward it as they go about their work. Sometimes this stems from the worry that applying one's work to the church makes it less than truly academic; other times it is the result of animosity toward the functional theology and practices of the church. At the same time, many people in the church adopt a similar attitude of detachment toward the work of theologians, much of which seems irrelevant or hostile to the church's daily life and mission.

This posture, along with tensions it produces, leaves each side frustrated with the other. Many Christians in the church worry that the discipline of theology is more beholden to the academy than to Christ,

---

[22]Ibid., 15.

and so they are suspicious about the content produced by academic theologians. This often leads them either to ignore academic theology or reject it. Academic theologians, in turn, often are exasperated with what they perceive as the simplistic faith of church members who hold views they consider to be unreflective and untenable. This drives theologians even deeper into the academy, with some of them seeing themselves as "nothing short of heroic in refusing to give the church what it wants."[23] Theology becomes more and more irrelevant to the life of the church, and the members of the church go about their business as if they do not need theology.

REBUILDING THE DISCIPLINE

The reality of the matter is that the church needs theology and theologians need the church. To untether the church from formal theological instruction is to give our functional theology free rein over our thinking and practice. This is a problem, and it remains so even if we try our best to adhere strictly to the teachings of Scripture. Because we inevitably interpret every word of Scripture in light of our presuppositions about the nature of God and reality, these presuppositions will determine what we think Scripture says and means. If we leave these presuppositions untested and unexamined, they are likely to be shaped not only by Scripture but also by our own ideals and the predominant currents of our age. If the church is going to think and speak rightly about God—and if it is not going to repeat the same theological errors generation after generation—then it needs the guidance provided by formal doctrinal instruction grounded in the history of the theological tradition.

Likewise, if we attempt to practice the discipline of theology in distinction from the life and work of the church, then the presuppositions governing the modern university likely will govern our theological method. Because the university assumes a framework of meaning and a criterion of rationality distinct from those presupposed within the Christian faith, the content of our theology is likely to become increas-

---

[23]Wolterstorff, "Travail of Theology in the Modern Academy," 37.

ingly divorced from this faith. Not only will this make our work less
relevant to the church, but also it will undermine the purpose of the
discipline. The traditional goal of Christian theology is to develop a
better understanding of God so that we can think and speak rightly
about God within the context of a life governed by our faith in Christ
and our discipleship to him in community with other Christians. Theology that proceeds from other grounds stands in tension with this goal.
If our claims are offered not with the end of knowing God or enabling
obedience to Christ but with the end of showing rational coherence, then
the most important thing becomes our ability to establish our right to
make these claims and to show that they stand together coherently. This
leaves theologians operating as if their primary goal is to defend the integrity of their own views. Practices like appealing to mystery or being
willing to retract one's views—both central to the traditional practice of
theology—become a sign of incompetence or weakness. At the same
time, spiritual practices such as prayer, worship and moral formation are
relegated to the realm of application, as if they have nothing to do with
our ability to think and speak about God rightly.

In this sense, Schleiermacher was right: the faith and practice of the
church cannot be separated from the academic study of theology. Our
challenge is to figure out what it looks like to bring them together so that
we can practice theology both faithfully and with intellectual integrity.
The latter emphasis means that we cannot turn back the clock and
practice theology as it was done in the past, before the pursuit of theology was linked to the practices of the university. And, in fact, the discipline of theology has benefitted greatly from the university and continues to do so. Theologians are better off when they have been trained
according to the highest standards of critical scholarship because this
training enables them to evaluate presuppositions, engage opposing arguments, examine the coherence and implications of their claims and
draw on the insights from other sources. To pull the discipline of theology out of the academy by making it solely an internal church enter-
prise would be unnecessary and unwise. We would be turning from the
multitude of gifts and opportunities God has given his church through

the university and undermining our ability to do our best theological work. There is no reason to assume that the practice of theology cannot be brought together with the highest standards of academic scholarship. The question is not whether theology also should be academic in character but how it should be.

The problem with Schleiermacher's approach is not that he brought the discipline of theology together with the standards of the university but that he worked in the wrong direction as he did so. He and other theologians across the entire theological spectrum allowed the assumptions of the modern university to set the parameters into which the discipline of theology must fit. Theologians had to begin their work by assuming the view of reality and history that governed the scientific disciplines that shaped the academic discourse within the university. This meant that theologians had to operate on the basis of a specific set of presuppositions about what counts as reasonable, what kind of claims can be justified and how arguments can be rightly made and defended. As a result, theologians had to practice their discipline from a distinctly non-theological starting point.

What if we worked in the other direction? What if we practiced theology in a way that corresponded to the highest academic qualities but according to the presuppositions of the Christian faith? To practice theology in this way, we would have to rebuild our conception of the discipline from the ground up. We would begin with the presupposition that the discipline of theology operates rightly when it proceeds on the basis of our faith in Jesus Christ. Our task would be to determine what counts as rational by starting with God's wisdom as it has been revealed in the saving work of Christ and the Holy Spirit. Then not only would we be able to connect the practice of theology to our life of discipleship, but we also could consider it to be a form of discipleship. Even the most academic of theologians could seek to embody the qualities and characteristics that go along with obedience to Christ, and they would seek to utilize their theological work to serve the life and mission of the church. At the same time, they would converse with the best insights of other disciplines in the university, both in order to learn from them and to contribute to them. This interdisciplinary conversation would not be in addition to the theologian's life of faith and service to the church but an integral part of it. By describing the discipline of theology in this way, we can offer an account of the practice of theology that overcomes many of the worries Christians have about it. Specifically, we can establish a framework from which we can practice theology in a way that is both academic *and* faithful by showing that our commitment to academic integrity and our faith in Jesus Christ do not exist in tension with one another.

The chapters that follow describe what it looks like to practice the discipline of theology in this way. Our starting point will be our confession that Jesus Christ is Lord and our belief that God raised him from the dead (Rom 10:9). We will work out the implications of this confession for our understanding of the nature of God, the content of God's wisdom and the order of created reality and history. On this basis, we will figure out what it looks like to live in relationship with God in light of the fact that Jesus Christ lives as the risen Lord. We then will seek to understand how God acts to shape our ideas and language so that we can think and speak about him rightly. Finally, we will describe key characteristics that distinguish theologians who practice theology within the context of a life of discipleship to Jesus. The goal of this rebuilding effort will be to show how a faithful theologian can be academically excellent and an academic theologian can be faithful.

two

BEING IN CHRIST

℘

"Follow me!" When Jesus Christ speaks these words to his disciples, he not only is calling them to a life of faith and obedience, but he also is unveiling their eternal destiny. The way of discipleship leads to eternal life with God because Jesus Christ is the incarnate Son of God. He shows us the truth about God and his plan for history by making us participants in God's wisdom and partners in this plan. The practice of theology is one form of this participation and partnership. The act of learning how to think and speak rightly about God is an act of faith and obedience that involves our participation in the mind of Christ and our partnership with Christ by the power of his Spirit. In this sense, the practice of theology takes place as an act of discipleship to Christ.

The next four chapters build a framework from which we can understand how and why the practice of theology can be an act of discipleship in this way. This chapter begins the process by showing how Christ gives us a new perspective on God's eternal being, his plan for history and the shape of our lives in relation to him. This perspective will enable us to see that the discipline of theology is ordered correctly when its central practices correspond to God's saving work in Christ and the Spirit. We think and speak rightly about God when we do so from the starting point of our faith in Jesus, which means measuring every claim about God by the implications of our confession that "Jesus is Lord" and our belief that "God raised him from the dead" (Rom 10:9).

But why should we begin from this starting point? What does our confession of faith in Christ imply about the nature of God and his relationship to human history? How does this confession help us understand our place in reality and history? And in what specific ways should it guide our practice of theology? This chapter addresses these questions in three sections: the first explores the implications of our faith in Christ for our knowledge of God and ourselves; the second discusses God's eternal plan for salvation history and its implications; and the third works out these implications for our practice of theology.

REFRAMING REALITY

A helpful place to start is with the visit of Paul and Barnabas to the Roman colony of Lystra. While preaching the gospel to the people of the city, Paul notices a disabled man who has the "faith to be healed" (Acts 14:9). Even though this man has never been able to walk, Paul tells him to stand up. Miraculously, the man arises. This miracle causes much excitement among the Lystrans, partly because they had heard about this sort of thing before. Greek and Roman literature contains many tales of gods performing miracles while disguised as human beings. For example, in one story, the Roman gods Jupiter and Mercury—known to the Greeks as Zeus and Hermes—wander the countryside pretending to be travelers looking for a place to rest. After being rejected repeatedly, they eventually find an older couple willing to invite them into their home. As the story goes on, this act of hospitality pays off for the couple, because it leads them to win the gods' favor and earn a special position of service.[1]

These kinds of tales prompted many in the ancient world to believe that the gods could show up on their doorstep at any moment. They knew that if they treated the gods well, great rewards might follow. This background may explain why the Lystrans react to the miracle as they do. They shout, "The gods have come down to us in human form!" (Acts 14:11), and they call Paul "Hermes" and Barnabas "Zeus." Before long, a

---

[1]For a discussion of this parallel from Ovid's *Metamorphoses*, see C. Kavin Rowe, *World Upside Down: Reading Acts in the Graeco-Roman Age* (New York: Oxford University Press, 2009), 20-21. My analysis on this point is drawn from his reading.

local priest comes to offer a sacrifice in their honor. The scene is both chaotic and comedic. Usually when Paul and Barnabas preach people try to kill them; this time, they are being worshiped as gods. The Lystrans are committing a classic case of mistaken identity.

Paul and Barnabas, however, do not see much to laugh about. As soon as they figure out that the people are worshiping them, they react in horror and tear their robes as a sign of blasphemy. They beg the crowd to stop, and Paul tries to correct their misunderstanding.

> Friends, why are you doing this? We are mortals just like you, and we bring you good news, that you should turn from these worthless things to the living God, who made the heaven and the earth and the sea and all that is in them. In past generations he allowed all the nations to follow their own ways; yet he has not left himself without a witness in doing good—giving you rains from heaven and fruitful seasons, and filling you with food and your hearts with joy. (Acts 14:15-17)

Here we see Paul addressing the Lystrans' misunderstanding by trying to help them recognize a key theological truth: God's divine being is infinitely distinct from all creaturely being. God is the Creator, the maker of all things; Paul and Barnabas are creatures, just like the Lystrans and everything else. God and creatures exist in completely different realms. By turning their worship toward created things, the Lystrans are not worshiping anything divine at all. Instead they are committing idolatry, exchanging "the glory of the immortal God for images resembling a mortal human being" (Rom 1:23). This false worship not only fails to benefit them, but also leaves them blind to the true nature of reality and their place in it.

This incident provides a fascinating case study as we consider how to proceed in the task of theology. Even though the true and living God reveals himself to the Lystrans through Paul and Barnabas, they fail to recognize him. Their problem is not that God gives them an inaccurate or incomplete picture of himself, or that Paul and Barnabas mislead them. They fail to receive God's revelation because their misguided functional theology prevents them from doing so. When God comes to them,

they interpret his revelation through the lens of their misplaced assumptions about the nature of divinity and how they should relate to it. This
leaves them blind to what is in front of them.

Although we may be tempted to dismiss the Lystrans' mistake as the
error of a superstitious and irrational people, we might be more like
them than we initially suspect. After all, every culture operates with a set
of basic assumptions about the nature of reality and history. We do not
live in a haphazard manner, thinking random thoughts and reacting to
events in unplanned and inconsistent ways. Rather, as rational beings,
we tend to think and act in coherent patterns that correspond to our
perception of the way things are. Our minds are shaped by a presupposed
framework of meaning, a picture of reality and history that puts the facts
and events of our lives in context and helps us decide how we should
think and act at any given moment. Thinking that corresponds to this
framework is considered rational, and actions that correspond to it are
considered moral. The Lystrans' presupposed framework of reality and
history included the possibility that gods like Zeus and Hermes might
enter into the created order and perform miracles. In light of these assumptions, certain patterns of thinking and behavior were expected and
encouraged. Their view of reality meant that if they witnessed a miracle,
it was probably the work of the gods. And their understanding of history
led them to believe that if a god revealed himself to them, the correct
course of action was to offer a sacrifice and try to win his favor. On their
own terms, the Lystrans responded to Paul's miracle in a rational and
moral way.

While very few of us adopt a framework of reality that includes figures
like Zeus and Hermes, we all operate with a set of assumptions about
reality and history that guide our thinking. For example, people in the
industrialized West tend to define reality and history in light of the idea
of progress.[2] We assume that history is moving toward something.
Things are rational and moral when they are moving toward something
better, and irrational and immoral when they are moving toward some-

---

[2]See N. T. Wright's remarks about "evolutionary optimism" in *Surprised by Hope: Rethinking
Heaven, the Resurrection and the Mission of the Church* (New York: HarperCollins, 2008), 81-87.

thing worse. On this basis, we believe that the world is ordered rightly when children are living healthier and happier lives than their parents, disease and poverty are becoming increasingly rare and technological innovation is leading us to more productive and comfortable lives. This kind of progress reflects the way things should be. We also tend to assume that people will live in a way that contributes to the greater good of everyone if they are given the freedom and opportunity to do so. Much of our political discourse corresponds to this assumption, and campaign promises and platforms are built around it. We shape our society and invest our resources on the basis of our expectation that, as the world becomes more educated and free, longstanding injustices, prejudices and abuses will become less prevalent. We promote thinking and action that correspond to this vision of reason and morality so that our society stands on the right side of history rather than being left behind.

Such goals are pursued with noble intentions. But how do we know that these assumptions are correct and that our efforts are not wasted? Certainly, the violence and suffering that occurred over the past century calls into question the idea that history is inevitably progressing toward something better. And is it really the case that, if left to our own devices, we will work for the benefit of others? Doesn't history suggest that the opposite might be true, and that our tendency is to work for our own benefit at the expense of others? Could it be that our modern assumptions about the way things are have been framed around our own projections of what we want to be true and what we wish to become? Could it be that we are just like the Lystrans? Have we been shaped by the ideals and assumptions of the culture in which we live to such an extent that we are blind to the true nature of God, reality and history despite the fact that God has been showing us the truth our entire lives?

Jesus' disciples illustrate how easy it is to fall into this kind of error. The Gospels repeatedly show that even though the disciples lived and worked closely with Jesus during his life, they did not grasp the truth about his identity or mission (Jn 12:16). Their misunderstanding did not stem from a simple mistake, as if they were merely confused or needed more information. Rather, they failed to grasp the truth about Jesus be-

cause they repeatedly misinterpreted his words and actions in light of
their own expectations and desires. Mark illustrates the depth of the
disciples' misunderstanding in a dramatic scene immediately following
Peter's initial declaration that Jesus is the Messiah (Mk 8:29-35). In response to Peter's confession, Jesus speaks openly about the nature of his
mission, revealing that he will experience great suffering, be rejected by
Israel's leaders, be killed and then be raised from the dead. These dire
predictions contradict Peter's vision for how the Messiah's life should
proceed, and so he begins to rebuke Jesus privately.

Peter's response gives us an interesting glimpse into the way that the
human mind operates. Peter's problem is not with what he knows about
Jesus, because Jesus himself has given him the right information. Rather,
Peter's problem is with how he interprets what he knows about Jesus. He
views Jesus in light of his own misplaced assumptions about what the
Messiah should be and do. Instead of allowing Jesus to reconfigure his
prior understanding of God and his plans, Peter tries to configure Jesus
to fit his own understanding. The nature of Peter's mistake helps us make
sense of Jesus' response to him: "Get behind me, Satan! For you are
setting your mind not on divine things but on human things" (Mk 8:33).
Peter's thinking is moving in the wrong direction. He is thinking from
below to above by starting with "human things" and then trying to make
Jesus correspond to them. Jesus calls him to think from above to below
by starting with God and then interpreting his life in light of who God
is and what God is doing in history.

The fact that the thinking of Peter and the other disciples is moving in
the wrong direction even as they live directly with Jesus shows that every
person, no matter how faithful or well-intentioned, is susceptible to the
same error. We are all like the Lystrans, and if we start with our presupposed picture of reality and try to fit God into it, we are likely to develop
an idolatrous picture of God. This tendency stems, in part, from the reality of our creaturely existence. As finite beings who live in a particular
time and place, we inevitably have a limited and partial perspective.
Thomas Aquinas emphasizes this point when he says that even though
we might be able to know some true things about God through the use

of our reason, this knowledge always contains "the admixture of many errors" because the truth of God exceeds our finite capacities.[3] These creaturely limitations are compounded by the effects of our sin. Paul emphasizes this point when he says that even though "what can be known about God is plain" to humans through "the things he has made," sin has caused them to become "futile in their thinking" (Rom 1:19-21). John Calvin draws upon this insight when he says that our thinking "neither approaches, nor strives toward, nor even takes a straight aim at, this truth: to understand what the true God is or what sort of God he wishes to be toward us."[4] As fallen beings with darkened minds, humans inevitably will picture God "as they have fashioned him in their own presumption" and thus worship "a figment and dream of their own heart."[5]

The remedy to these tendencies is to define the way things are in light of God rather than ourselves. As Dietrich Bonhoeffer puts it, "theological thought goes from God to reality, not from reality to God."[6] We have to make sure that the framework of meaning by which we decide what it means to be rational and moral corresponds to who God is and what God intends for our lives. But what does it look like to approach reality and history in light of God rather than ourselves?

Paul addresses this question during his speech to the Athenians in Acts 17. Disturbed by the idols on display in Athens, he begins to tell the people about Jesus. His preaching eventually causes enough commotion that he is brought before the city council. There he argues that God is utterly distinct from created being and thus beyond the ability of any human to define or imagine. "The God who made the world and everything in it, he who is Lord of heaven and earth, does not live in shrines made by human hands, nor is he served by human hands, as though he needed anything, since he himself gives to all mortals life and breath and

[3] Aquinas, *Summa Theologica* I, q. 1, a. 1.
[4] John Calvin, *Institutes of the Christian Religion*, 2.2.18, Library of Christian Classics 20, trans. Ford Lewis Battles, ed. John T. McNeill (Philadelphia: Westminster Press, 1960). This translation is the source of quotations from the *Institutes* in this book.
[5] Ibid., 1.4.1.
[6] Dietrich Bonhoeffer, *Act and Being: Transcendental Philosophy and Ontology in Systematic Theology*, Dietrich Bonhoeffer Works, vol. 2, ed. Wayne Whitsun Floyd and Hans-Richard Reuter (Minneapolis: Fortress, 1996), 89.

all things" (Acts 17:24-25). This same God has been actively overseeing the world, and "he is not far from each one of us." Paul notes that the Athenians have grasped this truth because they have realized that we are God's "offspring" and thus "live and move and have our being" in God. Even so, Paul says, their understanding remains faulty because they have been able to picture God only according to the "imagination of mortals." The good news is that they now can know the truth about God because God has been revealed in Jesus Christ. He stands at the center of reality and history because he has been appointed the judge of the entire world. This status has been verified by the fact God has raised him from the dead. The proper response to the risen Jesus, Paul says, is to repent from one's sin and follow him in faith (Acts 17:27-31).

Note the similarity between this argument and the one Paul made to the Lystrans. In both cases, Paul asks his listeners to turn from their mistaken assumptions rooted in the error of identifying God too closely with creation. Rather than depicting God within the limits of their own creaturely ideals, they need to realize that God exists in an utterly distinct way from creation. They are right to believe that God always has been present with them. The Lystrans have received God's good gifts in every rain shower, meal and happy moment, while the Athenians have experienced God's nearness through his direction of the history of their nation and their individual lives. But Paul challenges them to recognize that this same God also has entered into created history in Jesus Christ. They should abandon their own self-derived perceptions of divinity and look to Christ in order to figure out the true nature of God, reality and history.

Paul's argument points us in the right direction as we determine what the faithful practice of theology looks like because there are clear parallels between the situations of the Lystrans, Athenians and contemporary theologians. In all three cases, human thinking about God has missed the mark because it has proceeded on the basis of presuppositions about the nature of God and reality derived primarily from reflection on created realities rather than the knowledge of God that comes through Jesus Christ. What would our thinking about God look like if we started with Christ instead?

GOD'S ETERNAL PLAN

The best way to address this question is to see how Scripture depicts the relationship between God's saving work in Christ and our lives as we live them within the context of created reality and history. One of the most helpful passages in this regard is Paul's summary of God's saving plan in Ephesians 1.

> Blessed be the God and Father of our Lord Jesus Christ, who has blessed us in Christ with every spiritual blessing in the heavenly places, just as he chose us in Christ before the foundation of the world to be holy and blameless before him in love. He destined us for adoption as his children through Jesus Christ, according to the good pleasure of his will, to the praise of his glorious grace that he freely bestowed on us in the Beloved. In him we have redemption through his blood, the forgiveness of our trespasses, according to the riches of his grace that he lavished on us. With all wisdom and insight he has made known to us the mystery of his will, according to his good pleasure that he set forth in Christ, as a plan for the fullness of time, to gather up all things in him, things in heaven and things on earth. In Christ we have also obtained an inheritance, having been destined according to the purpose of him who accomplishes all things according to his counsel and will, so that we, who were the first to set our hope on Christ, might live for the praise of his glory. In him you also, when you had heard the word of truth, the gospel of your salvation, and had believed in him, were marked with the seal of the promised Holy Spirit; this is the pledge of our inheritance toward redemption as God's own people, to the praise of his glory. (Eph 1:3-14)

The key to interpreting this passage is to read it through the lens of Paul's statement about the blessings God gives to us. The content of these blessings corresponds to God's plan for our lives: he wants us to share in his eternal love as his adopted children. This future is our "inheritance," and God makes sure we will receive it by sending his Son to redeem us from our sins and his Spirit to seal our salvation by giving us faith in Christ and the ability to live "for the praise of his glory." The distribution of these blessings happens as the result of God's decision: "he chose us in Christ." As the one who chooses, God is the subject who establishes our relationship with him, and we are the object of his action along with Christ, who serves as our mediator. The gospel gives us the "the word of truth" about reality and history, a word "set forth in Christ" as the revelation of God's divine "wisdom and insight." Because we hear and know this truth of Christ by God's action alone, it remains a "mystery" beyond our comprehension.

We can unpack these ideas by turning to the striking series of phrases Paul employs to describe God's decision to save us. He says that God chose us "before the foundation of the world" and that God distributes his blessings to us "according to the good pleasure of his will," by the work of his "wisdom and insight," as a "plan for the fullness of time" and "according to the purpose of him who causes all things according to his counsel and will." These phrases cascade together, one after the other, to emphasize a single point: God's decision is not the result of a whim or an accident but of God's own wise plan for history. Even though God does not need us— and even though we rebelled against him in sin—God has decided to unite himself to us in Christ and the Spirit. He does so not as a backup plan or an emergency repair mission but out of his divine love and in line with his eternal knowledge and wisdom. God has decided to be our God, and he has decided that we will be his people. This is the truth revealed in the gospel: because God loves us, he has decided not to be God without us.[7]

In light of these emphases, we can affirm four key insights about the nature of God's decision to save us. First, it comes as a free and wise decision. When Paul says that God's choice to save us came "before the foundation of the world" (Eph 1:4), he is indicating that God made this choice before anything other than God existed. This takes us back to the two claims Paul made in his speeches to the Lystrans and Athenians: God is the creator of everything that exists, and God's divine being is infinitely distinct from all creaturely being. If these claims are true—and if God's being does not change over time (Jas 1:17)—then God must not need to relate to creation in order to be himself, because God was the unchanging God that he is before anything else existed. Or, to put it another way: God

---

[7]See Karl Barth, *Church Dogmatics* IV/1 (Edinburgh: T&T Clark, 1956), 7. Much of this section is drawn from Barth's insights.

is self-sufficient. He does not need anything in order to be the God that he is, and he would be the same God that he is if creation did not exist or if it existed differently than it does. God's self-sufficiency means that when God decided to save us "before the foundation of the world," he did not do so from a desire to gain something or because some internal or external obligation constrained him.[8] Rather, when God chooses to save us, he does so freely "according to his good pleasure" (Eph 1:9). This does not mean that God makes this decision randomly. God never acts in an incoherent way (1 Cor 14:33), nor does he act unwisely (Job 12:13). His decisions are always purposeful and in accordance with his own eternal wisdom. And unlike a human who has to deliberate about what he or she will do in a given moment, God's decisions are part of his eternal knowledge of his own being. Because God knows himself perfectly, he also has perfect foreknowledge of what he plans to do, including all the things he plans to do by exercising his will within the history of his creation. As Paul puts it, God's act to save us took place "with all wisdom and insight" and "according to his counsel and will" (Eph 1:8, 11).

Second, God's decision to save us reveals that God is a loving God. If God's acts are always purposeful, then his act to save us must have been performed for a specific purpose. Fortunately, Jesus explains this purpose to us: "For God so loved the world that he gave his only Son, so that everyone who believes in him may not perish but may have eternal life. Indeed, God did not send the Son into the world to condemn the world, but in order that the world might be saved through him" (Jn 3:16-17). This makes God's motivations clear: he saves us so that we might have eternal life, and he does so because he loves us. Because we know this act of love happened freely and purposefully in line with God's wisdom, we also know that it does not contradict God's being or character. Indeed, it would be absurd to believe that God would freely and intentionally act contrary to his nature. God is always faithful and true to himself. When God acts to save us out of love, this act expresses his true divine being and character.[9] As John puts it, "God is love" (1 Jn 4:8).

---

[8]See Aquinas, *Summa Theologica* I, q. 44, a. 4, ad. 1.
[9]Karl Barth, *Church Dogmatics* II/1 (Edinburgh: T&T Clark, 1957), 283.

Third, God's decision to save us unveils our eternal destiny. An event is predestined when it occurs as the result of God's decision that it take place in the way that it does.[10] When Paul says that God "destined us for adoption as his children through Jesus Christ" (Eph 1:5), he is saying that our lives always have been determined by this divine plan. The best way to understand this idea is to see it in light of the way that God has actually worked out this plan over the course of salvation history. Before creation, when God decided that he would adopt us as his children, he already knew that our sin would leave us living like "children of wrath" rather than children of God (Eph 2:3). This is why God chose us *in Christ*. Because God knew that we would need to be saved rather than merely created, he determined that his adoption plan would be accomplished through the saving history of the life of Jesus. "He was destined before the foundation of the world," Peter says, "but was revealed at the end of the ages for your sake" (1 Pet 1:20). Christ's life brings salvation because he comes as the second Adam, a new representative for humanity who establishes a distinct trajectory for our lives (1 Cor 15:22).

This trajectory runs through the incarnation. Even though God created and sustains all things through Christ, he takes our human "flesh and blood" as his own in Christ (Heb 1:1-2; 2:14). As he takes on our flesh, Christ incorporates our lives into his own, much like a branch on a vine (Jn 15:4-7). He unites the history of our creaturely lives to the history of his eternal life, and he dedicates himself to living for us and our salvation. He does so preeminently in and through his atoning death on the cross (1 Jn 4:10). God's goal in sending Christ to the cross was not simply to perform the act of atonement itself, as if it were its own end. He performed this act *for us*. Because the consequence of our sin is death—and because God's will is for us to live eternally as his beloved children—Christ bore our sin in our place so that we would not die but live with God for eternity. God verifies Christ's saving work on the cross by raising Christ from the dead. With this act, God irrevocably unites the history of his own eternal life together with the history of our lives, because now

---

[10]Aquinas, *Summa Theologica* III, q. 24, a. 1.

the Son of God will live his own eternal life in a resurrected human body.[11] This secures our righteousness before God, since anyone who has been united to Christ by faith will be counted just as righteous before God as he is (Rom 4:24–5:2). "For our sake," Paul says, "he made him to be sin who knew no sin, so that in him we might become the righteousness of God" (2 Cor 5:21).

In Christ we have been given a new status and a new history, one that spans from eternity to eternity. Christ's resurrection means that our present and future lives are no longer determined by what we have done but by what he will do for us. Freed from the power of sin and death, we now live under the promise that we "will certainly be united with him in a resurrection like his" (Rom 6:5). God has sealed this promise by giving us his Spirit, who serves as its guarantee. "If the Spirit of him who raised Jesus from the dead dwells in you," Paul says, "he who raised Christ from the dead will give life to your mortal bodies also through his Spirit that dwells in you" (Rom 8:11). Christ and the Spirit have given us a "new birth into a living hope," which is the prospect of our imminent adoption into God's family (1 Pet 1:3). Yet because we were destined for this adoption from before the foundation of the world, this new birth does not redefine us as much as it reveals what we always have been destined to become by God's grace. "For we are what he has made us," Paul says, "created in Christ Jesus for good works, which God prepared beforehand to be our way of life" (Eph 2:10).

Fourth, God's decision to save us reveals the truth about created reality and history. Because everything God does corresponds to his divine wisdom, his acts of creation and salvation both stand in line with his eternal plan. Paul makes this point when he says that "it is the God who said, 'Let light shine out of darkness,' who has shone in our hearts to give the light of the knowledge of the glory of God in the face of Jesus Christ" (2 Cor 4:6). The God who spoke all things into existence is the same God who saves his people through the incarnate Christ, and so creation must be seen in relation to Christ and vice versa. Because Christ is one and the same as God,

---

[11]See Barth, *Church Dogmatics* IV/1, 7-8.

however, the relationship between Christ and creation is an ordered relationship. "He is the image of the invisible God," Paul says, "the firstborn of all creation; for in him all things in heaven and on earth were created, things visible and invisible, whether thrones or dominions or rulers or powers—all things have been created through him and for him. He himself is before all things, and in him all things hold together" (Col 1:15-17). Paul's point is that Christ precedes creation and intrinsically determines its existence. As the eternal God, he is infinitely distinct from all created being: he comes before all things, and all things hold together in him because he sustains all things (cf. Jn 1:3; Heb 1:2-3). At the same time, he is the "firstborn of creation" because before God acted to create anything, he had already decided to save us through Christ's incarnate life. God created the world with the human birth of the eternal Son in his mind, and so the world cannot be understood in distinction from the specific history of Christ's union with our human nature. As Dietrich Bonhoeffer puts it: "When God in Jesus Christ claims space in the world—even space in a stable because 'there was no other place in the inn'—God embraces the whole reality of the world in this narrow space and reveals its ultimate foundation."[12]

The incarnation of Jesus Christ means that we cannot think about the way things are merely by looking at the facts of created reality and history and then reflecting on what we see. This approach would work if created being could be defined in distinction from God and his saving plan. But creation does not exist independently of God, as if it occupied its own space on the one side with God staying in his space on the other. Nor does creation exist in distinction from the purpose for which God made it or the history of God's actions within it. God revealed this purpose in the history of Jesus Christ's life. His incarnation is not just another event that can be defined in terms of the natural possibilities of created being itself.[13] Christ enters uniquely within creation, breaking into history from the outside in a miraculous act of God. And in doing so, Christ unveils

---

[12]Dietrich Bonhoeffer, *Ethics*, Dietrich Bonhoeffer Works, vol. 6, ed. Clifford Green (Minneapolis: Fortress, 2005), 63.

[13]See Ian A. McFarland, *From Nothing: A Theology of Creation* (Louisville, KY: Westminster John Knox, 2014), 37.

the content of "the plan of the mystery hidden for ages in God who created all things" (Eph 3:9). Nothing in creation stands outside the context of this saving plan. Any time we think about created reality and history, we also have to think about the history of Christ's eternal life. To fail to do so is to misunderstand the nature of creation altogether.

This insight is working behind the contrast Paul draws between the "wisdom of this age or of the rulers of this age" and "God's wisdom, secret and hidden, which God decreed before the ages for our glory" (1 Cor 2:7). His point is that the true history of creation runs through the manger to the cross and the empty tomb. "The history of salvation is *the* history," Karl Barth says, "the true history which encloses all other history and to which in some way all other history belongs."[14] In this sense, God's revelation in Jesus Christ reconfigures our understanding of everything. When we see the world through the lens of Christ, we see the truth about reality. We recognize that as the crucified and resurrected one, Christ stands "far above all rule and authority and power and dominion, and above every name that is named" (Eph 1:21). And we see that—because God has put "all things under his feet and has made him the head over all things"— Christ alone determines history's meaning and outcome (Eph 1:22). In the same way that Paul linked our changed perception of Christ—"even though we once knew Christ from a human point of view, we know him no longer in that way"—to our changed perception of ourselves—"from now on, therefore, we regard no one from a human point of view" (2 Cor 5:16)—so too does our understanding of reality and history change in light of our faith in Christ. He reveals God's purpose for creation: it is the space and the place made in, through and for him so that he might perform his work for our salvation. His life reveals the content of God's eternal wisdom most clearly (1 Cor 1:24). And so when we confess with Paul that the whole of creation reflects the "wisdom and knowledge of God" because "from him and through him and to him are all things" (Rom 11:33, 36), we also can say that the history of Christ's eternal life determines the trajectory from which, through which and to which all things in creation are moving.

---

[14]Karl Barth, *Church Dogmatics* III/1 (Edinburgh: T&T Clark, 1958), 60.

THEOLOGY BY PARTICIPATION

These claims about Jesus Christ's relationship to creation lead us to a key question: If the knowledge of Christ is the key to establishing a framework of meaning from which we can understand God, reality and history correctly, then how do we come to know Christ? Scripture makes it clear that until the day we see Jesus Christ face to face (1 Jn 3:2), we know him only by faith, which comes as the result of the hearing of the gospel. The gospel is the message containing the "good news" about Christ's identity and actions. Paul describes it as the "gospel concerning [God's] Son, who was descended from David according to the flesh and was declared to be Son of God with power according to the spirit of holiness by resurrection from the dead, Jesus Christ our Lord" (Rom 1:3-4). The *news* is that the eternal Son of God had come in the flesh as the heir of David, the Messiah of Israel; this news is *good* because God promised that Israel's Messiah would bring salvation by atoning for the sins of God's people and enabling them to live holy lives. This salvation becomes "effective through faith" in Jesus (Rom 3:25).

Paul describes the content of our faith in the following way: "if you confess with your lips that Jesus is Lord and believe in your heart that God raised him from the dead, you will be saved" (Rom 10:9). To confess that "Jesus is Lord" is to say that Jesus is one and the same as God. To believe that "God raised him from the dead" is to hold that Jesus is the *living* God who remains active in history from his seat at the right hand of the Father. It is to believe that we encounter Jesus not merely as a figure of the historical past but as a living and active subject at work in our lives in the present. This matches Paul's description of him as "Christ Jesus, who died, yes, who was raised, who is at the right hand of God, who indeed intercedes for us" (Rom 8:34). Christ intercedes for us, in part, through his Spirit, whom both he and the Father send to us to be the agent of Christ's presence in our lives. The Spirit dwells within us as a guarantee that God will relate to us into the future in fulfillment of the promise that we will be Christ's "joint heirs" and members of his own divine family (Rom 8:16-17). The familial nature of our salvation reflects the fact that God is a personal being. When we confess that Jesus is Lord,

we are saying that God is not something but someone. He has not remained distant from us or left us to figure out the truth on our own, but
he has made himself available to us so we might know him personally.
He has done so preeminently in Jesus himself, who shows us the truth
about God's divine being and character (Heb 1:2).

Our faith in Jesus Christ is undergirded by the reality that God always
acts in a way that is true and faithful to himself. Paul emphasizes this
point when he connects our faith to the fact that God "never lies" and
always keeps his promises (Tit 1:1-2). God does not deceive us, as if what
he shows us in Jesus somehow contradicts his true character or there are
other aspects of his life that remain undisclosed. God's being is not di-
visible in this way, as if there were distinct sides of his nature different
from one another. And because God never lies, there is no such thing as
a partial or half-true revelation: he either reveals himself as the true God
he is or he does not reveal himself at all. We may be sure that in Jesus
Christ "the whole fullness of deity dwells bodily" (Col 2:9). This affirmation is essential, because to say otherwise undermines our confidence
in the gospel. If Jesus Christ does not reveal the whole truth about God—
as if God's true being and character is something other than what Christ
shows us—then how can we be sure that "in Christ God was reconciling
the world to himself" (2 Cor 5:19)? How can we know that our faith in
Christ is not in vain? Our hope for salvation rests on the assurance that
God himself is at work in Christ and that Christ's saving work corresponds to God's will and fulfills his promises (2 Cor 1:20). If we think that
Christ does not tell us the truth about God, then salvation is placed back
in our own hands, because we are left to develop a picture of what God
is like on other terms and then fit Christ into that picture. This relativizes
Christ by making his life and actions secondary to our own ideas about
God and salvation. As a result, we end up in the same position as the
Lystrans, whose false assumption about divinity left them making vain
efforts to win the favor of idols.

The key to avoiding this kind of idolatry is to base our ideas about God's
being and character on our confession that Jesus Christ is Lord. Instead
of trying to fit God's revelation in Christ into our own prior understanding

of what God must be like, we have to allow our understanding of God to be determined by what Christ reveals about him. As Barth puts it, "we cannot discern the being of God in any other way than by looking where God himself gives us himself to see, and therefore by looking at his works, at this relation and attitude—in the confidence that in these his works we do not have to do with any others, but with his works and therefore with God himself, with his being as God."[15] This confidence is one of the key implications of the gospel. To confess that Jesus Christ is Lord is to believe that God's saving work in Christ faithfully displays God's true attitude toward us. Christ is not simply a good teacher or helpful example but "the way, the truth, and the life" and thus the standard by which our thinking and speaking about God must be measured (Jn 14:6).

Even as we affirm the truthfulness of God's revelation in Christ, however, we also have to recognize that the truth about God remains a mystery beyond our comprehension. God's revelation in created reality and history does not erase his difference from his creatures, and his divine being remains distinct from created being even as the Son takes on human flesh in Jesus. Among other things, this distinction means that God's revelation cannot be understood strictly on natural terms, as if it could be known like any other fact of history. God reveals himself in Christ, but Christ is a revelation of *God*, and his being still transcends our finite capacities. Paul reflects this idea when he describes Christ as "God's mystery" (Col 2:2). We know God truly in Christ, but Christ shows us that God is wholly different from any divine being we could have imagined. He makes this same point in 1 Corinthians 2, where he confidently proclaims that the crucified Christ reveals the truth about God and salvation while also insisting that Christ reveals "the mystery of God" and that God's wisdom in Christ contradicts "the wisdom of this age." His point is that while Christ shows us the truth, we cannot understand this truth on our own terms. Our knowledge of God comes as a gift from God, one we receive through the power of the Spirit as he shares his own knowledge of the "depths of God" with us (1 Cor 2:1-13).

---

[15]Barth, *Church Dogmatics* II/1, 261.

This insight helps us understand Paul's statement that we understand the things of God "dimly" and "only in part" in this life (1 Cor 13:12). He is *not* saying that there are hidden parts of God's being that God has yet to reveal. Rather, he is emphasizing that God remains beyond our comprehension even as we know him truly in Christ. He is making the same point when he exclaims, "O the depth of the riches and wisdom and knowledge of God! How unsearchable are his judgments and how inscrutable his ways!" (Rom 11:33). This claim is not about the nature of God's revelation but our inability to grasp it. Even as God reveals himself to us wholly and truly in Christ, the revelation comes to us as a miracle from outside our existence. Christ shows us that our lives have been determined not by the whims of history or the possibilities inherent to us but by God from before the foundation of the world. And because God is utterly distinct from us and has determined every part of our lives from before our existence, he remains beyond our ability to comprehend fully.

But if God remains a mystery even in Christ, how we can be sure that the knowledge of God we have in Christ is true and accurate? The best way to answer this question is to show how God's revelation in Christ— and the knowledge of God we have through Christ by the power of the Spirit—relates to the inner life of God. Specifically, because we know God only because he has revealed himself to us in Christ and the Spirit, we need to figure out how this revelation relates to God's eternal being. This leads us to the doctrine of the Trinity. Our task is to figure out how we can know the truth about God's incomprehensible divine being as a result of his relationship with us within the context of created history.

A helpful place to start as we consider this task is with Galatians 4, where Paul describes God's plan to adopt us as his children through Christ and the Spirit.

> But when the fullness of time had come, God sent his Son, born of a woman, born under the law, in order to redeem those who were under the law, so that we might receive adoption as children. And because you are children, God has sent the Spirit of his Son into our hearts, crying, "Abba! Father!" So you are no longer a slave but a child, and if a child then also an heir, through God. (Gal 4:4-7)

Note how Paul embeds our knowledge of God—signified by the Spirit giving us the ability to know God as "Father"—within the context of the saving actions of Christ and the Spirit. His depiction of these actions takes the form of a narrative with a trinitarian plot: in accordance with his eternal plan, God the Father sent his Son and Spirit into the world so that, through the Son's redeeming work and the Spirit's transforming power, we might be adopted as children of the Father. The trinitarian shape of this plot makes sense when we consider that, unlike us, God always acts in perfect correspondence to his being. We do not always live in line with who we are. Sometimes we lie about ourselves, put on a false face in front of others or act against our own better judgment. God never does these things. He always acts in a way that is faithful and true to his own being and character. And because God is triune, it makes sense that his actions in history take place in a trinitarian pattern that corresponds to the order of the eternal relationships between the Father, Son and Holy Spirit. Because the Son eternally proceeds from the Father, and the Spirit eternally proceeds from both the Father and the Son, God's actions follow the same pattern: they originate from the will of the Father, proceed through the Son and are made effective by the power of the Spirit.

This pattern is working in Paul's description of our adoption through the Son and Spirit. His presupposition is that the actions of the Son and the Spirit bring salvation because they correspond to God's will both for his life and ours. God is not acting randomly or from necessity but freely in line with his plan for "the fullness of time." This means that when the Son and the Spirit act for our salvation, the one God is acting. Or, to put it in trinitarian terms: when we see the Son in the midst of his mission to save us, we are seeing the Son living out his eternal relationships with the Father and the Spirit within the context of created history; likewise, when we see the Spirit in the midst of his mission to indwell and empower us, we are seeing the Spirit living out his eternal relationships with the Father and the Son within the context of this same history.

Recognizing these trinitarian patterns puts us in position to grasp two important implications of Paul's passage. First, God's saving actions in

Christ and the Spirit show us that God's plan is to make us participants in his own divine life. This is precisely how Paul depicts it: God redeems us from our sin by sending his Son so that we can exist *in* him and thus share his relationship with the Father through the power of the Spirit. As a result of the saving work of Christ and the Spirit, we truly are given "a part in the being of God."[16] This does not mean that we *become* God, as if we cease to be creatures and are absorbed into God's life. It means that our lives are "hidden with Christ in God" (Col 3:3). The central reality of our existence is that God has united himself to us in his Son so that we can live in, with and through the Son as he lives his eternal life in relation to the Father by the Spirit.

Second, our participation in God through Christ serves as the basis of our knowledge of God. As the Spirit gives us a share in Christ's relationship with the Father, he also gives us a share in the Son's own knowledge of his Father—"Abba! Father!"—in line with God's plan. This matches Jesus' description of how we come to know God. He says that he was sent by the Father to speak the Father's words and then give them to us (Jn 17:8, 18), and he also teaches that he and the Father will send the Spirit to enable us to understand him rightly (Jn 14:16; 15:26). These claims correspond to the distinct order of the triune God's actions: the Father wills that the Son speak his words to us; the Son speaks these words in line with the Father's will; and the Spirit enables us to understand the Son's words and thus know the Father through the Son. Each of these three moments stands along a single trajectory of divine movement involving the Father, the Son and the Spirit, and God perfectly corresponds to himself in each moment. When the Father sends the Son to speak his words, God is living out the eternal relationship of the Father and the Son in created time; when the Son speaks these words, he is living out his own eternal relationship with the Father; and when the Spirit comes to us from the Father and the Son, he is living his one divine life in relation to them both. We hear and know the Word of God as a result of the actions of the one triune God—Father, Son and Spirit.

---

[16]Barth, *Church Dogmatics* IV/1, 8.

And these actions show us that God has dedicated himself to making us creaturely participants in his divine life so that we can know him. God the Father sent his Son into history to join himself to us so we could live in union with him by the power of the Spirit. As we do so, we participate in the Son's divine knowledge, which is one and the same as God's knowledge of himself. This fulfills God's decision to adopt us as his children and give us a share of his divine inheritance. God wants his adopted children to know their Father, and he sends his Son and Spirit on a saving mission to make sure this happens.

The fact that our knowledge of God comes through participation in Christ by the Spirit explains why we can be confident in it. We know that our knowledge of God is true because it reflects the eternal Son's own knowledge of God. The fact that we have this knowledge by participation in Christ, however, means that it always remains beyond our control or grasp. After all, participating in Christ is not the same thing as *being* Christ. He knows God by nature because he is God by nature; we know God as finite and temporal creatures who have been given a share in Christ's mind by grace. In this sense, we are much like a passenger who gets picked up by a train halfway through the train's journey. On the one hand, the passenger truly participates in the train's journey and has accurate knowledge of both the train and its movement toward its destination. On the other hand, the passenger's knowledge is "only in part" because she has participated in only part of the journey: the train and its journey long preceded her participation in it, and she has not yet arrived at the destination and has no direct knowledge of it. Something similar happens when we are given a share in Christ's mind through the saving missions of Christ and the Spirit. In line with God's eternal decision, Christ breaks into history and unites his life to ours so that we can live in and through him; and the Spirit pours forth his power within us so that we can live with Christ and share in his mind. We are caught up together with the Son and the Spirit as they work out God's saving plan for our salvation so that we become participants in God's life through them. This participation gives us true knowledge of God and his plan. But, because we remain finite creatures who have been made participants in God and his eternal plan, this knowledge remains beyond our ability to comprehend fully. One day, we will reach our final destination and stand before the throne of God as joint heirs with Christ in the love of the Spirit. Then, the veil of mystery will be removed, and our true knowledge will become more complete. "For now," Paul says, "we see in a mirror, dimly, but then we will see face to face. Now I know only in part; then I will know fully, even as I have been fully known" (1 Cor 13:12). Until that day arrives, the knowledge of God we have through Christ and the Spirit remains mysterious even as it is true.

This account of how we know God by our participation in the life of God through Christ and the Spirit helps us begin to make sense of how we should approach the practice of theology. The discipline of theology proceeds rightly when it begins from the presupposition that all right thinking and speaking about God, reality and history takes its bearings from the life of the incarnate Jesus Christ. Our thinking about God has to follow after him, because our knowledge of God takes place in and through him. This starting point corresponds to Paul's instructions that we are to "seek the things that are above, where Christ is, seated at the right hand of God" (Col 3:1). Any right account of reality will begin with the person of Jesus; any true story of history will start with the history of what he has done; and wisdom and reason are called such only when they correspond to his own. To start our thinking with Christ does not mean that we have to withdraw from the world in which we live, as if we now have to abandon any insights drawn from elsewhere. We do not need to make "a total surrender of the wisdom which is either innate or acquired by long experience," Calvin insists, but rather, we need to hold this wisdom lightly and with a willingness "to yield to God and to embrace with fear and reverence whatever He teaches rather than to follow what seems acceptable to us."[17] This corresponds to John's instructions that we are to "test the spirits to see whether they are from God" by discerning whether they line up to the fact "that Jesus Christ has come in the flesh" (1 Jn 4:1-2). To know reality in light of Christ is finally to know the way

---

[17]John Calvin, *Commentary on 1 Corinthians* 3:18, from *The First Epistle of Paul the Apostle to the Corinthians*, trans. John W. Frazer (Grand Rapids: Eerdmans, 1960), 80.

things are, and to interpret history within the context of his eternal life is to see the meaning and significance of every event from the perspective of God's wisdom rather than our own. We are able to adopt this perspective through the instruction of the Holy Spirit, because he is the one who makes us participants in Christ's own divine wisdom. "The Son is Wisdom itself," Athanasius says, "and so when we receive the Spirit of Wisdom, we possess the Son and become wise in him."[18] This stands in line with Paul's statement that the Spirit shows us the "depths of God" by making us participants in the "mind of Christ" himself (1 Cor 2:10-16). Our participation in Christ's mind is how our fallen minds are "renewed in knowledge according to the image of [our] creator" (Col 3:10), and this is the precise renewal we need in order to think and speak about God rightly as theologians.

Our need for this renewal corresponds to Paul's claims to the Lystrans and Athenians: whatever assumptions we hold about reality and history—and whatever ideas we have about God and our own lives—must be reinterpreted in light of the living God, the one revealed to us in the Christ we embrace by faith through the power of the Spirit. As Bonhoeffer puts it, the "whole reality of the world has already been drawn into and is held together in Christ" such that history "moves only from this center and toward this center."[19] We cannot place Christ into other frames of reference or other systems of meaning without denying his true status and projecting false images on him. When we confess faith in Christ we are confessing that the history of his eternal life serves as the context from which *everything* is understood.

[18]Athanasius, *Letters to Serapion* 1.19.5, in *Works on the Spirit*, trans. Mark DelCogliano, Andrew Radde-Gallwitz and Lewis Ayres (Crestwood, NY: St. Vladimir's Seminary Press, 2011).
[19]Bonhoeffer, *Ethics*, 58.

- three -

PARTNERSHIP WITH CHRIST

☞

To confess faith in Jesus Christ is to believe that we live within the context of a divine decision. God has decided that, despite our sin, he would spare us from death and equip us to live eternally as his adopted children. The central truth of our existence is not that we have been created by God or sinned against him but that God has decided to save us in Christ. We are the people for whom Christ lived and died; and we are the people who, because we are united with Christ, will be raised to stand with him before the Father in the power of his Spirit. This is our true identity. We are the people whose lives find coherence within the context of the divine plan that runs through the eternal life of the incarnate Son of God.

God's decision also shapes how we live. We not only "have our being" in God but "live and move" in him as well (Acts 17:28). Our human lives should reflect the pattern of his divine life, such that our thoughts, speech and actions move in the same direction that God is moving. And this means moving in the direction *Christ* is moving. As "the beginning and end" of all things (Rev 21:6), Jesus does not merely stand at the center of created history but moves within it as its Lord, determining it as he goes. "Christ does not find himself indolently resting at his place," Karl Barth says, but "strides through the ages still left to the world until his final return in its final form."[1] Christ's ongoing movement in history

---

[1]Karl Barth, *Church Dogmatics* IV/3.2 (Edinburgh: T&T Clark, 1961), 663.

helps us understand what it means to say that "all things hold together" in him (Col 1:17). Christ exercises his lordship in that he personally holds created reality together as he continues to act within it by his Spirit to bring about God's plan for history.

The gospel tells us that Christ does not do this work without us but that he has united himself to us by his Spirit. This union means that we have been incorporated not only into the past and future history of his life but into his present life as well. Paul depicts this reality when he says, "I have been crucified with Christ; and it is no longer I who live, but it is Christ who lives in me. And the life I now live in the flesh I live by faith in the Son of God, who loved me and gave himself for me" (Gal 2:19-20). Christ bore the consequences of our sin on the cross, but he also lives in and through us now, such that we exist as members of his own body (Eph 5:30). God has "made us alive together with Christ" (Eph 2:5). And because Christ lives an active existence, our life with him is active. We have not been united to Christ to live as mere spectators to his work; we have been united to him to live as his partners.

We understand the nature of our partnership with Christ only when we see his life within the context of the history of God's plan to adopt us as his children. This history takes a covenantal form, because it has been shaped by God's promises to his people and their promises to him in return. Jesus Christ stands at the center of this history because he is the one who keeps the covenantal promises on both the divine and the human sides. This is why his life determines our relationship with God. It also explains why Christ's life determines the proper practice of theology. Theologians are people who partner with Christ to bring finite human ideas into correspondence with God's eternal being by learning how to "take every thought captive to obey Christ" (2 Cor 10:5). We do this work through the power of the Spirit, who works through Scripture as well as the church to help us think and speak rightly about God.

THE PATTERN OF PARTNERSHIP

To understand the nature of our theological partnership with God, we need to understand what God created humans to become. This means starting with our creation in the image and likeness of God. When read within the context of the entire Bible, it is clear that when God spoke the words, "Let us make humankind in our image, according to our likeness" (Gen 1:26), he had Jesus Christ in mind. That is to say, before God acted to create us, he had already decided to save us in and through Christ so that we could live as his adopted children for eternity (Eph 1:4-5). We understand what it means to be in the image and likeness of God only when we see ourselves in light of this decision and the history that flows from it.

The first thing God's decision shows us is that God creates us in order to establish a relationship with us. God is a personal God, and he made us as personal subjects so that we can relate to him within the context of the history he lives together with us. This means that we can be ourselves only by living together with God. After all, while we are made in God's image, we are not the divine image itself, and so we need to live in relation with God to be what we were made to be.[2] We also need to relate to others. Because our relationship with God is shaped by his desire to adopt *children*, we live in God's image when we exist together with God's people. This is reflected by the corporate nature of the image: "So God created humankind in his image, in the image of God he created them; male and female he created them" (Gen 1:27). There is no such thing as a human who images God in isolation.

This is where our creation in the likeness of God comes in. If our being in the image of God is determined by our relationships with God and others, then the way we exist is just as important as the fact that we exist. We are defined primarily not by the capacities we possess but by the way we use our capacities within the context of our relationships.[3] We learn how to use our capacities rightly by looking to the particular way the incarnate Jesus utilizes them as he lives his own human life in perfect relation to God and others. We understand Jesus' life rightly, however, only when we view it in light of the history of his mission to save us. This history forms the bulk of Scripture. The entire canon of Scripture, both

[2]See Kathryn Tanner, *Christ the Key* (New York: Cambridge University Press, 2010), 12.
[3]See Robert Jenson, *Systematic Theology*, vol. 2: *The Works of God* (New York: Oxford University Press, 1999), 146-47.

Old and New Testaments, testifies to both how and why Christ is the key
to our relationship with God and thus to our humanity. As we read
Scripture in light of our relationship with Christ, we see that God created
us to be what we are destined to become as a result of the history of
Christ's eternal life.

This history begins in Eden. When God puts Adam in the garden to
"till it and keep it," his plan is for Adam to join Eve in exercising "dominion" over creation (Gen 2:15; Ps 8:6-8). This dominion does not in-
volve domination but oversight. God gives Adam and Eve authority over
creation so they can "image," or reflect, his own loving divine being
within the world by bringing order to a chaotic creation.[4] And God does
not just leave them to figure out how to perform this task on their own.
He helps them by partnering with them as they go about their work. We
see this partnership in action, for example, when God allows Adam to
name the animals. God's prior act of speaking the animals into existence
is followed by Adam's subsequent act of speaking their names, and together these two actions bring order to creation in line with God's intention (Gen 1:20-21; 2:19-20). Here we see the pattern of God's partnership with us: God's divine action enables us to offer a corresponding
human action that moves toward a single divine goal.

God's purpose in establishing his partnership with us is to enable us to
relate to him as members of his own family. He gives us specific respon-
sibilities because he wants us to act in a way that corresponds to his divine
being and character. And just as a parent teaches a child about how a
member of the family should live, so God gives us instructions about how
we should think and act in relation to him. This is what he does with
Adam and Eve in the garden. God makes himself personally available to
them and teaches them about how they should live, including about the
trees from which they should and should not eat (Gen 2:16-17). God's goal
in giving these commandments is not subservience but likeness. He wants
Adam and Eve to live in correspondence to his plan for their lives so they

[4]See Basil the Great, "On the Origin of Humanity: Discourse 1: On That Which Is According to
the Image," in *On the Human Condition*, trans. Nonna Verna Harrison (Crestwood, NY: St. Vladimir's Seminary Press, 2005), 36-42.

can reflect his divine wisdom and character as they partner with him in their oversight of creation. This partnership prefigures the eternal life they will spend with him as his adopted children.

The problem is that even though God partners with Adam and Eve, they try to live without him. When the serpent tells them that eating the forbidden fruit will make them "like God, knowing good and evil" (Gen 3:5), he knows that these two elements—being "like God" and "knowing good and evil"—are intrinsically related. He is offering them a chance to be "like God" without having to relate to God or rely on his instructions. Once they have the ability to determine good and evil for themselves, they will gain autonomy from God and his plan. This offer presents Adam and Eve with a decision. Will they trust God's wisdom by obeying his commands, or will they make their own judgments and choose their own future? Will they live as members of God's family, or will they go their own way?

Their decision to disobey God and embrace their own path breaks their relationship with God. It does so because, by trying to become "like God" on their own terms, they are abandoning the true likeness to God that comes through the act of partnering with him. Because the whole of creation was ordered around God's plan to establish this partnership, their abandonment of it leaves them with disordered lives. Adam and Eve reflect this disorder immediately after they sin. Instead of meeting God when he comes to them in the garden, they hide in shame (Gen 3:8). Then, once their sin becomes public, their lives are turned upside down. God informs them that the earth will be cursed rather than enriched by them, and instead of overseeing creation, they will be buried within it after a lifetime of toil (Gen 3:17-19). Worse still, they are cast out of God's presence so they no longer have immediate access to him (Gen 3:22-24). Not only will Adam and Eve be unable to relate to God as they once did, but also they will be a shell of their former selves. Apart from God's direction, they will live a distorted existence and become disfigured versions of what they were created to be.

This disfigurement is magnified in their immediate descendants. Rather than living as God's partners and family members, humans began to live such that "every inclination of the thoughts of their hearts was only evil continually" (Gen 6:5). Paul later applies this inclination to every human when he says that even though we were made to know and relate to God, our sin has left our minds "darkened" and "senseless" so that we continually "suppress the truth" (Rom 1:18, 21). We spend our lives groping for something that lies beyond us, unable to know God as he planned. The result is idolatry. "Claiming to be wise, they became fools," Paul says, "and they exchanged the glory of the immortal God for images resembling a mortal human being. . . . They exchanged the truth about God for a lie and worshiped and served the creature rather than the Creator" (Rom 1:22-23, 25). This great reversal shows how far humans have fallen from God's original intention. Instead of knowing God personally, we create false gods that are little more than shallow images of ourselves. And rather than partnering with God in the oversight of creation, we choose to worship and serve created things as if they were divine. Instead of heading toward eternal life with God as his children, therefore, our lives are aimed toward a "day of wrath, when God's righteous judgment will be revealed" (Rom 2:5).

Because this outcome contradicts God's plan for our lives, God acts to reverse it by reestablishing his partnership with humanity. He does so by making a covenant with his chosen people, the people of Israel. A covenant is an elective partnership with obligations on both sides. God's covenant with the people of Israel begins with his promise to Abraham. God tells him that he will form a "great nation" from his descendants and bless "all the families of the earth" through them (Gen 12:1-3). God commits himself to this promise with a sacrificial oath (Gen 15:7-21), and Abraham's commitment to God is sealed through an act of obedience, his circumcision (Gen 17:1-8). Abraham's descendants become the people of Israel when they claim these promises and commitments as their own by affirming their own covenant with God after he saves them from slavery in Egypt. Israel vows to obey God's commandments, and God promises that if they do so, they will be his "treasured possession" and a "priestly kingdom and a holy nation" (Ex 19:5-6). This way of life prefigures God's plan for eternity: God will "dwell among" his people so they can know and partner with him as he works out his plan for history (Ex 29:46).

God frames his relationship with Israel personally, as is shown by the way he explains his first commandment to them on Mount Sinai:

> Then God spoke all these words: "I am the LORD your God, who brought you out of the land of Egypt, out of the house of slavery; you shall have no other gods before me.
>
> You shall not make for yourself an idol, whether in the form of anything that is in heaven above, or that is on the earth beneath, or that is in the water under the earth. You shall not bow down to them or worship them; for I the LORD your God am a jealous God, punishing children for the iniquity of parents, to the third and the fourth generation of those who reject me, but showing steadfast love to the thousandth generation of those who love me and keep my commandments." (Ex 20:1-6)

Note how God follows the pattern established in Eden. He makes himself available to his people and gives them commandments about how to live rightly with him. These commandments are embedded within the context of his personal relationship with them—*you* and *me*—because God wants Israel to be clear about why he wants them to obey his words.[5] He saved them so they can receive his "steadfast love" forever. He wants their obedience because he wants to live together with them, to partner with them in the fulfillment of his plan for history. To help them do so, God will equip them by blessing them as far into the future as they can imagine. The statements about idolatry and punishment fit into this context. God wants his people to live with *him*, and to turn toward idols is to turn away from him. Idolatry is a personal matter for God because God is jealous for his people. He wants a familial relationship with them, and he rejects anything that threatens it.

Despite God's faithfulness to his covenant promises to Israel, however, much of the Old Testament tells the story of Israel's repeated rejection of their covenant with God. Their disobedience leads God to punish them and call them to repentance. Eventually, their failures prompt an

---

[5]See Karl Barth, "The First Commandment as an Axiom of Theology," in *The Way of Theology in Karl Barth: Essays and Comments*, ed. H. Martin Rumscheidt (Allison Park, PA: Pickwick Publications, 1968), 63-78.

accommodation: God allows them to install a human king who can embody the kind of partnership God wants with his people. The king's task is to obey God's commands and lead the people to do so as well. David stands as the preeminent example of a king who faithfully executes this task, and God promises to relate to him and his heirs like a father to a son (2 Sam 7:14). As a sign of this relationship, God promises that these heirs will build a temple for God that will represent God's permanent partnership with Israel. As the years pass, however, the kingly heirs of David repeatedly reject God, and together with the people, they embrace the gods of the nations instead. In response, God calls down his wrath on Israel, culminating this time in the destruction of the temple, the exile of the people from their land and the unraveling of their partnership with God.

These are the events that set the stage for the incarnation of Jesus Christ. In the midst of Israel's exile, God speaks through the prophets to issue promises of restoration that signify once again that he will not permit sin to thwart his plan to adopt his people as his children. The prophets tell Israel that God will lead a new exodus to "recover the remnant that is left of his people" in exile (Is 11:11). God also will raise up a Messiah, a new heir to David's throne, who will atone for the people's sins, renew their covenant with God and fulfill God's plan for the whole of creation. This Messiah will reign with God's wisdom and live according to God's justice and righteousness (Jer 23:5). And this time, the people will obey God because God will empower them to do so by his own Spirit: "I will put my spirit within you, and make you follow my statues and be careful to observe my ordinances" (Ezek 36:27). This gift will seal their obedience because they now will think and act with God's own power as they live in partnership with him.

The prophets' promises about the coming Messiah and the gift of the Spirit are heard again with the birth of Jesus. The angel Gabriel links the unborn Jesus to these promises by telling Mary that her child would be "the Son of the Most High" and occupy "the throne of his ancestor David" (Lk 1:32). This is confirmed by the prophet Simeon, who proclaims that Jesus will be "a light for revelation" (Lk 2:32), and by John the Baptist, who tells his followers that Jesus "will baptize you with the Holy Spirit and fire" (Lk 3:16). Jesus himself begins his ministry by declaring that the "time is fulfilled, and the kingdom of God has come near" and that God's promised restoration has been fulfilled in him (Mk 1:15; Lk 4:12). He calls twelve followers in a symbolic reconstitution of the tribes of Israel (Mk 3:13-14), identifies himself directly with God's temple (Jn 2:19) and proclaims that he has come to fulfill God's commandments (Mt 5:17). He also claims God's promise of the Spirit by saying that he will ask his Father to send his disciples the "Spirit of truth," who will come to dwell in them (Jn 14:16-17).

The legitimacy of Christ's identification with these divine promises is confirmed when, after his crucifixion, death and burial, he is raised from the dead and "declared to be Son of God with power according to the spirit of holiness" (Rom 1:4). Jesus then appears to his disciples and tells them to wait for the gift of the Spirit: "I am sending upon you what my Father promised; so stay here in the city until you have been clothed with power from on high" (Lk 24:49). This power arrives after Jesus' ascension, when all the believers are "filled with the Holy Spirit" during Pentecost and form the church (Acts 2:4).

On the basis of this fulfillment of God's promises about the Messiah and the Spirit, the apostles claim that Jesus was the "substance" of the grace given to Israel in the prior centuries and the fulfillment of God's original promise to Abraham (Col 2:17). Just as God had always intended, God's blessing is now available to all peoples through Israel, and specifically through Israel's Messiah as he reigns as the King of kings who draws anyone who has faith in him into partnership with God through the power of his Spirit. Peter's first proclamation of the gospel captures all of these elements: "Repent, and be baptized every one of you in the name of Jesus Christ so that your sins may be forgiven; and you will receive the gift of the Holy Spirit. For the promise is for you, for your children, and for all who are far away, everyone whom the Lord our God calls to him" (Acts 2:38-39).

This biblical history running from Adam through Israel to Christ and the church indwelled by his Spirit tells us the story of how God establishes his partnership with us. From before the foundation of the world, God knew that his decision to adopt us as his children would be fulfilled through this specific history and through the Son who stands at the center of it. This biblical history is *our* history, because it tells the story of how we will become what God created us to be. We do so through Jesus Christ—the new Adam, the true descendant of Abraham and David, the Messiah of Israel and our brother in the flesh.

LIFE WITH CHRIST

Paul emphasizes Christ's brotherhood with us in his account of God's saving work in Romans 8. This passage is unique among Paul's summaries of God's saving plan in Christ because of the specific way that Paul links our present relationship to God with our destiny to live eternally as members of God's divine family.

> We know that all things work together for good for those who love God, who are called according to his purpose. For those whom he foreknew he also predestined to be conformed to the image of his Son, in order that he might be the firstborn within a large family. And those whom he predestined he also called; and those whom he called he also justified; and those whom he justified he also glorified. What then are we to say about these things? If God is for us, who is against us? He who did not withhold his own Son, but gave him up for all of us, will he not with him also give us everything else? (Rom 8:28-32)

As he does elsewhere, Paul emphasizes that God's saving work in Christ stems from God's sovereign decision and reflects his love as well as his perfect knowledge, wisdom and purpose. Yet Paul's focus here is less on the nature of God's decision than its implications. He explains that God predestined us to reach a specific goal: conformity to the image of his Son. This goal corresponds to his plan to adopt us. Children adopted into a family are expected to participate in the life of the family. In our case, we do so by bearing the image of the firstborn Son so that we can share in his own intimate relationship with the Father by the Spirit. Our conformity to Christ brings our human nature to its fulfillment, because it brings us into correspondence with the destiny for which we were created. Paul connects this predestination to God's acts of calling, justifying and glorifying us. He believes that these actions are effective in conforming us to Christ precisely because God is the one who performs them. Who is going to thwart God, he asks, especially when he also has given his own Son in order to achieve the same goal? We can understand how these divine actions conform us to Christ by following the chain of action from calling to justification to glorification.

The fact that God calls us into conformity with Christ reveals that this conformity involves our active participation in the life of Christ. God relates to us as personal subjects, and we maintain our integrity even as he unites us to Christ. Our human nature is not undermined, because Christ's human life reveals what God always intended our human nature to become. He created us with rational minds and physical bodies knowing that he would save us through Christ's assumption of a human mind and body. The Spirit conforms us to Christ by uniting us to him, giving us a share in his mind and guaranteeing that our bodies will be raised like his body so that we can live with God forever (1 Cor 2:16; Rom 8:11). All of this brings our human nature to its destiny: we were created precisely so that we could be shaped into the image of the incarnate Son and share in his eternal life before the Father by the Spirit.

The problem is that our sin has left us both unwilling and incapable of responding to God's call. So, those whom God calls he also justifies. To be justified is to be set right so that we no longer stand guilty before God because of our sin. Jesus serves as the key to our justification by fulfilling the requirements of the law on our behalf during his life while also bearing the consequences of our sin in our place through his death. This life means that Jesus himself is our righteousness, and he is raised from the dead so that we might be justified by being united to him (1 Cor 1:30; Rom 4:25). Christ's righteousness is imparted to us as the Spirit unites us to him by grace as a result of our faith in him. Because of this union, we are not merely called righteous but *are* righteous before God. "We experience such participation in him," John Calvin explains, "that although we are still foolish in ourselves, he is our wisdom before God; while we are sinners, he is our righteousness; while we are unclean, he is our purity; while we are weak, we were unarmed and exposed to Satan, yet ours is that power which has been given him in heaven . . . while we still bear about with us the body of death, he is yet our life."[6] The result of our righteousness in Christ is freedom. We no longer stand condemned, or fear the power of sin and death, because we live our own lives in and through his life by the power of his Spirit (Rom 8:1-2).

The fact that we do not contribute to our own righteousness does not contradict God's plan to bring us into conformity to Christ's image. Rather, it shows us what conformity to Christ involves. We are not conformed to Christ by performing righteous deeds, as if we need to reach some Christ-like standard. We are conformed to Christ when he makes us participants in his life. Or, to put it another way: God did not predestine us to do something so that we could become like Jesus; he predestined us to become someone in Jesus and thus do things like him. Paul describes this as being "clothed" with a "new self," one that has been "renewed in knowledge" and shaped "according to the likeness of God in true righteousness and holiness" (Eph 4:22-24; Col 3:9-10). This new self involves our being "clothed" with Christ as we live in union with him (Gal 3:27-28). We play our part in this union through our faith, which is the mode of our participation in Christ. Our faith involves our whole-hearted trust that our relationship with Christ is not only real but also eternal and thus definitive for our whole existence.[7] We place our entire identity—past, present and future—into his hands and see our lives through the lens of his eternal being and saving mission. We do so knowing that his life is the sole basis for our "hope of sharing in the glory of God" (Rom 5:2).

This leads to the final link in the chain: those whom God justifies he also glorifies. The nature of our glorification can be explained through Paul's remark that our salvation stems from "God's wisdom, secret and hidden, which God decreed before the ages for our glory" (1 Cor 2:7). When he says that God's decree is for *our* glory, he does not mean God's plan is to glorify us in the sense that we end up on a higher level than

---

[6]Calvin, *Institutes of the Christian Religion*, 3.15.5.
[7]See Jenson, *Systematic Theology*, 2:68-72.

God. He means that God makes us participants in *his* glory, which is the good and perfect life he eternally lives as Father, Son and Spirit. God glorifies us so that, through our participation in Christ by the power of the Spirit, we can actively partner with God as he works out his eternal plan for history.

Our uninhibited partnership with God will take place when we are made like Christ and our sinful bodies are "conformed to the body of his glory" (Phil 3:21). This will happen only in the future when we will work together with him in the new heaven and new earth (Rev 21:1-3). We can begin to live in line with this future, however, by partnering with Christ in the present. Paul gestures in this direction when he connects our future life with Christ to our present state of being: "for you have died, and your life is hidden with Christ in God. When Christ who is your life is revealed, then you also will be revealed with him in glory" (Col 3:3-4). His point is that the risen Jesus, who shares a perfect relationship with the Father in the Spirit, lives the eternal life of God. Because we exist in Christ, we are hidden participants with Christ in the life of God. While our own place in this life will not be unveiled until the future, we experience a foretaste of it now as Christ lives in and through us. Paul's rhetorical question, "Do you not realize that Jesus Christ is in you?" (2 Cor 13:5)—as well as his statement "it is no longer I who live, but it is Christ who lives in me" (Gal 2:20)—both capture the present-tense nature of this reality.

Peter develops the implications of our life with Christ when he explains that Christ's "divine power" leads us to "become participants of the divine nature" (2 Pet 1:3-4). The Greek word translated into English as "participants" is *koinonia*, which can also be translated as "fellowship," "partnership," "communion" or "sharing." These various translations help us understand the implication of Peter's claim: our partnership with Christ is the way we participate in the life of God. Despite our sin, we are able to live together with God in and through Christ as he continues to work out God's plan for history. Peter explains that as we live with Christ, he empowers us to move us away from sin by giving us specific virtues that conform to his own divine way of life. Christ's power strengthens our faith with goodness, which itself is enriched by our Christ-propelled growth in knowledge, self-control, endurance, godliness, mutual affection and love. The presence of these virtues confirms our calling and election by God, and they enable us to be effective and fruitful partners with Christ in anticipation of our future "entry into the eternal kingdom" (2 Pet 1:5-11).

The conviction undergirding these claims is that the history of Jesus Christ's life as the eternal Son of God—which includes the history of his life and death as well as the history of the life he continues to live as the resurrected Son of God—has become our history because he has joined his life to ours. What happened to him in the past happened to us, because our lives have been incorporated into his own. His life now takes place with us and, in part, through us, so that as we live in him through the power of his Spirit, we are participating in the life of God. We have become "holy partners in a heavenly calling" together with Christ (Heb 3:1).

The fact that we have to be called, justified and glorified so that we can enter into this partnership means that Christ leads the way within it (Eph 4:15). This is where discipleship comes in: we partner with Christ by following after him. Christ acts freely in line with God's eternal wisdom and divine will; we follow him in obedience by conforming our actions to his own. Our actions within the partnership thus are made possible by Christ's prior actions. This does not make our actions unimportant, as if we make no real contribution to the working out of God's eternal plan. No—just as Adam and Eve played an important role in God's plan to bring order in creation, so we have an important role to play in salvation history as we partner with Christ. In fact, because Christ acts precisely in order to lead us in our partnership with him, the production of our action is a central part of Christ's own work in salvation history. Christ's obedience takes place in part through the production of our obedience. However, because our obedient actions are determined and enclosed by Christ's action, our actions always take place together with him. Christ's action to lead us—and our acts of obedience in response to him—forms a single history of divine action performed by Christ in and through us in line with God's plan for history.

The reality that Christ directs our partnership such that our actions are incorporated into his own does not mean that we lose our identity in him. Even as we participate in Christ—and even as Christ calls, equips and enables us to follow him in obedience by the indwelling power of his Spirit—we remain distinct from him and act with our own integrity. Nor does Christ lose himself in us, as if he somehow becomes less than truly God or is robbed of his glory as he lives his own life and works his own ministry through us. We are not in competition with Christ, nor he with us, because the goal of his faithful obedience is to produce our faithful obedience in return. Christ united himself to us precisely so that we can live obediently with him in line with God's intention. The "righteousness of God," Paul says, "is revealed through faith for faith" (Rom 1:17).

A helpful way to understand both how Christ leads us and the effects that our partnership with him has on our lives is to examine Paul's use of the word *koinonia* to describe our relationship with Christ and the Spirit. As was the case in Peter's usage of this term, Paul employs this word to indicate that two parties exist in such close partnership or fellowship that they mutually participate in one another. He typically uses it whenever he wants to describe a relationship between two persons who live and act as one even as they remain distinct.[8]

For example, he talks about how God's act of calling us "into the fellowship (*koinonia*) of his Son" enriches us in "speech and knowledge of every kind" and strengthens us "to the end" so that we live "blameless" lives (1 Cor 1:5-9). Here Paul depicts God as the primary actor, and he has acted by uniting us to his Son so that we can know and obey him by living in accordance with his plan. This is a brief description of God's saving work in history: God's action to unite us to Christ transforms us so that we can enter into a true partnership with God. In this sense, our *koinonia* with Christ both serves as shorthand for the story of our salvation and reflects the nature of Christ's relationship with us. On the one

---

[8]See George Hunsinger, "The Mediator of Communion: Karl Barth's Doctrine of the Holy Spirit," in *Disruptive Grace: Studies in the Theology of Karl Barth* (Grand Rapids: Eerdmans, 2000), 168-73. The account of *koinonia* offered here is indebted to his insights.

hand, as the living Lord who sits at the right hand of the Father, Christ remains above earthly history and so is not controlled or limited by it in any way. On the other hand, because he is the Lord who became incarnate for the sake of our salvation, Christ does not remain separated from history as if he were "the prisoner of his own height and distance."[9] Rather, he fills "all things," including our own lives (Eph 4:10), as he incorporates us into his life so that we can have a real and living partnership with him through the Spirit.

Paul sees the transformative effect of our partnership with Christ as something that grows exponentially over time. As the Spirit works to conform our lives to Christ by ushering us more deeply into "the knowledge of God's will in all spiritual wisdom and understanding," this knowledge prompts us to "lead lives worthy of the Lord" that "bear fruit in every good work" (Col 1:9-10). Our good works multiply as the Spirit brings our efforts into concert with the Spirit-inspired works of other Christians who also are partnering with Christ. Together we form the church, the covenant people of God who have the "communion (*koinonia*) of the Holy Spirit" (2 Cor 13:13) as well as a "sharing (*koinonia*) in the Spirit" (Phil 2:1). Our *koinonia* with the Spirit and one another does not mean losing our individuality but expressing it in and through our relationships with God and others. In this way, our partnership with other believers enriches our participation in God's life and plan. And because this plan stems from God's love and his desire that we share in this love as his children, we display our conformity to Christ and live in line with our eternal destiny as we learn to love our fellow Christians and partner with them to love the world (Gal 5:22). As we partner with God and others, the Spirit works to conform us to the image of Christ (2 Cor 3:18). He transforms our minds by prompting us to follow Christ in obedience. We begin to remove "every proud obstacle raised up against the knowledge of God" and start to "take every thought captive" to Christ (2 Cor 10:5). At the same time, he enables us to present our bodies as a "living sacrifice" to God (Rom 12:1-2). The result is that our entire lives

---

[9] Karl Barth, *Church Dogmatics* IV/2 (Edinburgh: T&T Clark, 1958), 653.

begin to correspond to God's intention for them. Through union with Christ and the transforming power of his Spirit, we begin to live as members of God's own family, reflecting his qualities and character in the way we think, speak and act.

THEOLOGY WITH CHRIST

This account of our partnership with God through Christ and the Spirit puts us in position to see how God enables us to contribute to the life and work of the church as theologians. We practice theology in order to guide the church as it thinks and speaks about God. This work is our specific commission. God has given us the task of bringing order to the church's language, and this task puts us in a position of service rather than superiority. We are responsible for directing the church so that its prayer, worship and preaching correspond to God's being and character. Our goal is to help the church become confident that its claims about God are true so it can teach believers within the church—and proclaim the gospel to those outside the church—in grace and truth.

The challenge we face as we go about this task is that the church has no choice but to use human words as it thinks and speaks about God. Because these words were originally derived and defined by finite human minds reflecting upon created realities, they are unfit to be applied directly to God. "We are human and he is the Lord our God," Herman Bavinck explains. "There is no name that fully expresses his being, no definition that captures him. He infinitely transcends our picture of him, our ideas, our language concerning him."[10] In other words, even as we are called to speak the truth about God, God's divine being remains infinitely distinct from creaturely being and is by nature "invisible" to us (Rom 1:20; 1 Tim 1:17). This puts us in a precarious position. We are called to perform a task that we are, by nature, incapable of performing. Even our best words fail us when it comes to speaking about God.

The intrinsic unfitness of our words is complicated by the reality that every word we use for God comes with a history of usage that shapes

---

[10]Herman Bavinck, *Reformed Dogmatics*, vol. 2: *God and Creation* (Grand Rapids: Eerdmans, 2004), 47.

its meaning long before we apply it to God. For example, consider the biblical claim that "God is love" (1 Jn 4:16). Prior to ever encountering this claim, we already have a functional idea of what *love* means. We have experienced love from before we could talk, and our lives are shaped by our love for various people and things. It would be a mistake, however, to assume that our common usage of *love* corresponds precisely to its meaning in the phrase "God is love." We could easily say the phrase "God is love" but express a meaning that reflects our creaturely ideals rather than the truth about God's divine being.[11] Doing so leaves us with a picture of God shaped around our own human experience—which would be an idol. But, of course, our words about God have to mean *something*. If the meaning of the word *love* in the phrase "God is love" has little or no connection to our normal use of it, then it is difficult to know what we are communicating when we say that phrase. The claim becomes meaningless. And if we say that no human word can ever rightly be applied to God, we are effectively saying that the limits of our language make God totally unknowable by us. Not only does this stand in tension with the idea that God reveals himself to us, but also it returns us to the precipice of idolatry. If all we can say about God is that his divine being is unknowable by us, then we are likely to identify God's being with the reality that exists at the limits of our own being and knowing. The result is that our creaturely existence once again sets the parameters for our description of God, and we are left with an idol.[12]

This is where theologians enter the picture. Our job is to help the church avoid these problems by showing how we can use human words for God without projecting creaturely ideals onto him. But how do we accomplish this task? A good place from which to address this question is John's description of the word *love* in 1 John 4. His insights provide a template for how we might offer similar instructions to the church as it applies this and other human words to God.

---

[11]See Aquinas, *Summa Theologica* I, q. 13, a. 1 and a. 2.
[12]On this point, see Barth, *Church Dogmatics* II/1 (Edinburgh: T&T Clark, 1957), 303-4.

Beloved, let us love one another, because love is from God; everyone who loves is born of God and knows God. Whoever does not love does not know God, for God is love. God's love was revealed among us in this way: God sent his only Son into the world so that we might live through him. In this is love, not that we loved God but that he loved us and sent his Son to be an atoning sacrifice for our sins. Beloved, since God loved us so much, we also ought to love one another. No one has ever seen God; if we love one another, God lives in us, and his love is perfected in us.

By this we know that we abide in him and he in us, because he has given us of his Spirit. And we have seen and do testify that the Father has sent his Son as the Savior of the world. God abides in those who confess that Jesus is the Son of God, and they abide in God. So we have known and believe the love that God has for us. (1 Jn 4:7-16)

John's goal in this passage is to help his readers love one another in the pattern of God's love, because he believes that this love is the key to knowing and living in communion with God. He realizes that, in order to accomplish this goal, he needs to draw a connection between God's love and our own human idea and experience of love. To make this connection, he instructs his readers about the true nature of God's love and then shows them how they can participate in it.

He begins by arguing that "love is from God" and a person who loves is "born of God and knows God." When we fail to love, we live in contradiction to God, because "God is love." We will know God rightly only when we love like God does. Two problems, however, prevent us loving God in this way. First, we do not know God rightly because he remains beyond us: "no one has ever seen God." How can we love like God if we do not understand him rightly? Second, our sin leaves us unable and unwilling to love in the way God intended. Even if we did know God, therefore, we would not love in the way he does.

The good news, John says, is that God overcomes both these problems by sending his Son to save us from our sins and give us new life. By doing so, he reveals the true nature of God's love. "In *this* is love," John says—not that we know what love is on our terms, but rather we know God's love through Christ. And John makes it clear that Jesus does not merely give us intellectual knowledge of God's love, as if he simply presents us with new information about it. Rather, he shows us God's love by making us active participants in it as we "live through him." This is the language of partnership: Christ shows us God's love by loving through us. As we partner with Christ and he loves through us, our understanding of love is reconfigured. This happens in two ways. First, as we live in Christ, he becomes the criterion by which we define the meaning of love. Our faulty ideas are exposed and judged by his life, so that we no longer think that we know what love is on our own terms. Second, as Christ lives in us, we learn about God's love by loving God and others through Christ's own power. This happens as the Spirit leads us to confess Christ and "abide in God" through him by sharing his own love for others.

John's depiction of the way we come to know God's love provides a template for our work as theologians. As we seek to obey our commission to guide the church in its use of words to think and speak about God, we have no choice but to use human words. We do so, however, knowing that we cannot apply them to God on our own terms. Rather, God himself must show us how to use them rightly, and he does so in and through Jesus Christ. Paul reflects this idea when he says that our "assured understanding" of God takes the form of our "knowledge of God's mystery, that is, Christ himself, in whom are hidden all the treasures of wisdom and knowledge" (Col 2:2-3). The paradoxical tension between understanding and mystery—with Christ himself standing in the center—indicates that even as we know the truth about God, we always do so on God's terms. He always remains beyond us as someone no human idea or word can fully capture. Even so, as those who confess that Jesus is Lord, we also believe that he entered into time and space and lived among us without compromising his divine being or character: "for in him the whole fullness of deity dwells bodily" (Col 2:9). As he lived his incarnate life, he employed created realities to reveal himself to us, and he continues to use them in his self-revelation as the resurrected and ascended Lord. On the basis of these actions, we know that even as God remains distinct from us—and even as our human words are still intrinsically unfit to be applied to God—we can rightly apply them to God as long we do so in line with the way God has done so in Christ. Our thinking and speaking about God will be true if our words correspond to who Christ is, what he has done and what he continues to do within created history.

This means that our primary task as theologians is to bring the meaning of the words we use for God into conformity to Christ. We measure each one by his being, actions, teaching and promises. If the meaning of a word as applied to God leads us to knowledge that corresponds to what we know of God in and through Christ, then we know that our use of this word is right and true. If the meaning does not correspond to what Christ shows us, then we know that we either have to refine the meaning of that word or stop using it in our speech about God. Although God remains "concealed from us in so far as these words are our words and not his own word about himself," Barth says, we talk rightly about him as long as we "allow [God] himself to be the interpreter of these human words which he has placed upon our lips."[13] We are guided in our interpretation by the Spirit of Christ, who leads us into the truth by teaching us how to think and speak in a way that matches what Christ has revealed (Jn 16:13).

To illustrate how this process of discernment works, consider the claim that God is *sovereign* (Ps 8:1). In our everyday usage, we typically employ the word *sovereign* to refer to human leaders, especially those who exercise power in the political sphere. Kings and queens are sovereign over their realms. As theologians, our task is to understand what the word *sovereign* means when we apply it to God so that we can guide the church to use this word rightly in its thinking and speaking about God. While we know that the meaning of *sovereign* will be similar to the meaning it has when applied to kings and queens—because God exercises authoritative power over his creation—we also know that it will not be identical. No human will be able to exercise his or her sovereign rule in exactly the same way God does, nor does God act precisely like a human ruler. To determine the nature of the difference, we look at the

---

[13]Barth, *Church Dogmatics* II/1, 336, translation revised. See Barth, *Kirchliche Dogmatik* II/1 (Zürich: Evangelischer Verlag, 1940), 377.

life of Jesus Christ within the context of the whole of Scripture. Our task is to figure out what it means for God to be *sovereign* on the basis of what Christ has revealed to us about the being and character of God.

When we do so, Christ challenges our everyday usage of the word, because he often acts in a way that contradicts our normal expectations of what it means to be sovereign. For example, we would not expect a king to take the role of a slave and demonstrate weakness before others, but this is precisely what Jesus does (Phil 2:7). We also know that kings and queens often use their sovereign rule for their own benefit, to gain something for themselves. Those who engage in extreme forms of this behavior we call dictators and tyrants. But Jesus shows us that God does not exercise his sovereign rule for his own benefit. In Christ, God acts sovereignly, not for himself but for others. In fact, he exercises his power with the goal of sharing his life and goodness with us by saving us from our sins at the expense of his own life. "You know that among the Gentiles those whom they recognize as their rulers lord it over them," Jesus says, "and their great ones are tyrants over them. But it is not so among you; but whoever wishes to become great among you must be your servant, and whoever wishes to be first among you must be slave of all. For the Son of Man came not to be served but to serve, and to give his life a ransom for many" (Mk 10:42-45).

These words, together with Christ's example, guide us as we learn what the word *sovereign* means as applied to God. We know that we are applying the word *sovereign* to God correctly when everything Jesus has shown us about God and his rule fits into our definition of the word. He shows us that God's sovereign rule includes acts like taking the form of a slave, working for the benefit of others, serving rather than being served and acting with self-sacrificial love. All of this transforms our understanding of the meaning of the word *sovereign* when used in theology. If we fail to measure the meaning of this word by Christ—that is, if we define God's sovereign rule on the basis of our human examples—then we are likely to come out with a picture of God that looks a lot like a human ruler who uses his power to "lord it over" his subjects and work for his own benefit. Christ shows us the error of this way of thinking. He shows us that the true God exercises his sovereign rule through sacrificial and self-giving love, and he does so for our sake.

Our task as theologians is to apply the same treatment to *every single word* we use for God. Doing so is part of the way we "take every thought captive to obey Christ" (2 Cor 10:5). We engage in this task with the conviction that, as we reconfigure the meaning of our words in light of Christ, our words are purified rather than distorted. This purification is part of Christ's intercessory work, and it reflects the reality that he is the criterion by which all things find their meaning because he is "the beginning and the end" of all things (Rev 22:13). This process also reflects God's plan "to gather up all things in him, things in heaven and things on earth" (Eph 1:10). To redefine our words in light of Christ is to gather them up, give them to him and trust he will lead us to use them in a way that corresponds to the eternal wisdom of God. As Barth puts it, by guiding our theological language, "Jesus Christ himself sees to it that in him and by him we are not outside but inside. . . . He sees to it that what is true in him in the height is and remains true in our depth."[14]

This means that we never practice theology alone. Christ works alongside with us, partnering with us so that we might better serve his body, the church. He does so by directing the use of our language so that we can think and speak such that our ideas and words correspond to the eternal being of God. Christ's direction can take a variety of forms, but he often works through the instruments of Scripture and the church. Long before we ever tried to apply words to God, the Holy Spirit was directing and leading the human authors of Scripture to record God's words and deeds so that they might serve as the means by which we understand God's saving plan. Christ sends that same Spirit to teach us the truth about him (Jn 14:26). The Spirit does so by helping us to see reality and history in light of this biblical narrative so we can understand the centrality of Christ to our lives and begin to conform our thinking to him. The Spirit also directs us by bringing us into relationship with other Christians, both living and dead, who also have heard and inter-

---

[14]Karl Barth, *Church Dogmatics* II/1, 156.

preted these same biblical words through his illuminating power. Their insights guide us as we consider how we might think and speak about God together with them as members of one church.

The next two chapters explore how Christ and the Spirit use Scripture and the church to direct our practice of theology. Taken together, the goal of these two chapters is to help us understand the nature of Christ's theological partnership with us so we then can discern what it means to live as faithful theological partners with him.

- four -

THE WORD OF GOD

✆

The previous chapters made the case that our lives take place within the context of God's plan to adopt us as his children. We become active participants in this plan as God unites us to Jesus Christ by his Holy Spirit. This union frees us from the consequences of our sin so that, through the Spirit's power, we can partner with Jesus in his ministry to the world. God equips us for this partnership by giving us new knowledge, which breaks into our minds like the sun through dark clouds. While we once lived ignorantly under a veil and were unable know God rightly, now "the veil is removed," and we are able to approach him "with unveiled faces, seeing the glory of the Lord as though reflected in a mirror" (2 Cor 3:16-18). This chapter offers an account of how God uses the Bible to remove this veil of ignorance and direct us in our partnership with Christ. That God does so is no accident. In his perfect wisdom, God ordained that he would employ human authors and texts to accomplish his divine plan and bring about our participation in it. The Bible exists so that, in obedience to the Father's will, the risen Jesus Christ can address his people and call them to be disciples who, through the power of his Spirit, follow him in faith and obedience as he partners with them in line with God's eternal plan.

The Bible's unique role in God's plan gives it a special place our lives, as reflected by the title we give it: *Holy* Scripture. To confess that the Bible is holy is to say that these texts have been set apart as God's speech to us.

Though written by human authors and composed with human words, they are effective with God's power and serve as the criterion for our thinking and speaking about him. The goal of this chapter is to show how God relates to Scripture and how it fits into God's plan for our lives. We will proceed by exploring how God relates to human words as he uses them within his sovereign plan. Then, by seeing how these words relate to Christ, we will draw some key implications that lay the groundwork for a vision of theology that corresponds to our life of discipleship to him.

GOD AND HUMAN WORDS

That God would accomplish his plan through words stands in line with his divine being and character. The apostle John emphasizes this point in the opening line of his Gospel: "In the beginning was the Word, and the Word was with God, and the Word was God" (Jn 1:1). This verse reaches behind the first chapter of Genesis into the eternal life of God. When John joins his two claims about the Word together—that the Word *was* God and the Word was *with* God—he implies that God himself is a God of words, and that communication is essential to his being as Father, Son and Spirit.[1]

God expresses his communicative nature as he relates to creation. This begins with his act of speaking it into existence. "By the word of the LORD the heavens were made, and all their host by the breath of his mouth," the psalmist says. "For he spoke, and it came to be; he commanded, and it stood firm" (Ps 33:6, 9). This pattern of action continues as God brings order to creation by naming and blessing it with words (Gen 1:5, 22). The New Testament connects God's use of words directly to Christ. "Long ago," Hebrews says, "God spoke to our ancestors in many and various ways by prophets, but in these last days he has spoken to us by a Son, whom he appointed heir of all things, through whom he also created the worlds" (Heb 1:1-2). Note the trajectory traced out in this passage: the same God who spoke creation into existence and then spoke through Israel's prophets now speaks through Jesus Christ. These divine actions—

---

[1]For a development of this point, see Scott Swain, *Trinity, Revelation and Reading: A Theological Introduction to the Bible and Its Interpretation* (London: T&T Clark, 2011), 16-17.

from creation to Israel to Jesus—take place along a single line of communication moving from God to us. The apostle John traces this same line when he draws a link between the Word through whom "all things came into being" and the Word who "became flesh and lived among us" (Jn 1:3, 14).

To confess that the Bible is God's Word is to say that it exists within this same trajectory of divine communication. It does so because God providentially decided to use it as an instrument through which he would accomplish his saving plan for history. That God chooses to do so indicates that, like every other created thing, Scripture's existence reflects God's perfect knowledge of himself and all things. As John Calvin puts it, God "has from the beginning" determined that he would bring about his plan by opening "his own most hallowed lips."[2] This helps us grasp what it means for us to come into contact with the words of the Bible. When we hear or read Scripture, we are not merely encountering human words recorded in ancient texts. We are encountering God's own speech. The same God who became incarnate in Jesus Christ and whose Spirit indwells us also speaks to us through the human words of Scripture.

We can make sense of how he does so by starting with the various ways believers encounter Christ and come to faith in him. In the New Testament, some people meet the risen Jesus through bodily means. The disciples, for example, believe in Jesus after he reveals himself to them, an event immediately linked to their reception of the Holy Spirit (Jn 20:20-22). The most famous example of this sort is the disciple Thomas, who would not believe until he could touch Jesus for himself (Jn 20:25-28). Jesus comes in a similarly direct way to Saul, who comes to faith after Christ confronts him on the road to Damascus (Acts 9:1-9).

Beyond a direct encounter, Jesus also meets believers through the testimony of authorized witnesses. During his ministry, Jesus said that the Spirit would "testify on my behalf" but also said that his disciples would do the same thing: "You also are to testify because you have been with me from the beginning" (Jn 15:26-27). Their testimony is linked to the

---

[2]Calvin, *Institutes of the Christian Religion*, 1.6.1.

presence of the Spirit in them. "When the Spirit of truth comes," Jesus says, "he will guide you into all the truth; for he will not speak on his own, but will speak whatever he hears, and he will declare to you the things that are to come" (Jn 16:13). Paul describes this as being "taught by the Spirit" (1 Cor 2:13), and he argues that this instruction makes his preaching "a demonstration of the Spirit and of power" rather than merely an example of his rhetorical skills (1 Cor 2:4). He links the presence of this power to his union with Christ, saying that those "in Christ" preach and speak "as persons sent from God and standing in his presence" (2 Cor 2:17). This implies that Christ's authorized witnesses are not simply passing along information or expressing their own opinions. Rather, God himself is speaking through them by the power of his Spirit. As their listeners listen to them speak, they are hearing God's own speech. Paul reflects this idea when he reminds the Thessalonians that "when you received the word of God that you heard from us, you accepted it not as a human word but as what it really is, God's word" (1 Thess 2:13). This is precisely what enables the preaching of Christ's witnesses to lead to salvation for those who hear. "You have been born anew," Peter says, "not of perishable but of imperishable seed, through the living and enduring Word of God," which comes through "the good news that was announced to you" (1 Pet 1:23, 25).

God's decision to speak through human words not only corresponds to his communicative being but also matches the way God ordered his relationship with us from the beginning. From our creation onward, God structures his life with us around the giving of words and our response to them. For example, we see this in Eden when God gives Adam and Eve verbal instructions and expects their obedience in return (Gen 2:16-17). Their sin against God involves their act of questioning God's words and then disobeying them (Gen 3:1). When God inaugurates his plan of salvation, he follows the pattern established in Eden. He initiates his covenant with Abraham, and later with the people of Israel, by speaking words to them and then expecting their obedience in return (Gen 12:2-3; Ex 19:3-8). In fact, the Israelites interpret their entire relationship with God through the lens of their reception of words from God: "one does not live by bread alone, but by every word that comes from the mouth of the LORD" (Deut 8:3).

The idea that God sets certain people apart to serve as instruments of his speech corresponds to God's desire to make us partners in his divine work. As the one who creates and sustains our existence, God has the power to order our lives so that our words, freely spoken by us in our own context, correspond to his eternal purposes. "Even before a word is on my tongue, O LORD," the psalmist says, "you know it completely. You hem me in, behind and before, and lay your hand upon me" (Ps 139:4-5). In line with his plan for salvation history, God equips certain people to speak his word at particular times in order to accomplish his will at that moment. God's gift of speech to Moses serves as a case in point. "Who gives speech to mortals?" God asks Moses. "Who makes them mute or deaf, seeing or blind? Is it not I, the LORD? Now go, and I will be with your mouth and teach you what you are to speak" (Ex 4:11-12). Moses' words are not identified with God because of any special ability Moses possesses, but because God has directed Moses' life so that his words will be identified with God's will and radiate his divine power. God later explains this process to Jeremiah: "Before I formed you in the womb I knew you, and before you were born I consecrated you; I appointed you a prophet to the nations. . . . I have put my words in your mouth" (Jer 1:5, 9). This same idea is working in the background of Peter's claim that those "moved by the Holy Spirit spoke from God" (2 Pet 1:21). Paul likewise identifies with this process when he says that God "set me apart before I was born and called me through his grace . . . so that I might proclaim him" (Gal 1:15-16).

As the church has considered this idea over time, theologians have been nearly unanimous in saying that God's act of setting apart certain people to serve as instruments of his divine speech does not detract or violate their integrity as creatures. God does not violently take over the minds and wills of the humans who speak for him, nor does he use them as passive instruments, as if they were mere stenographers dictating his words. Instead, God speaks perfectly in and through his human agents even as they retain their own creaturely integrity.

Thomas Aquinas provides an example of the traditional approach to the relationship between divine and human action that undergirds this idea. He argues that because every created thing lives, moves and has its being in God (Acts 17:28), "God is necessarily internally present in any active thing, active in it, as it were, when he moves it to act."[3] This means that every creaturely action takes place through the presence and power of God.[4] This reality does not render human actions meaningless, as if God were the sole and direct cause of everything a human does. Humans can and do act freely in accordance with their rational capacities. They do so because God works out his providential plan by means of interme-diate secondary causes that can occur contingently, meaning that they can take place in accordance with or in contradiction to God's good will.[5] Free human actions fall into this category. That they do so does not mean that these actions happen outside the context of God's providential plan or threaten its fulfillment. Aquinas explains that because the human agent performing the contingent action exists only as a result of God's divine action—and because the human action itself occurs within the context of God's sovereign plan for history—"the contingency of effects or causes cannot disturb the certainty of divine providence." In other words, God sovereignly accomplishes his one divine plan for history pre-cisely in and through the contingent free actions of human beings. We can be sure that the result of these actions will accord with God's plan because of the "infallibility of the divine foreknowledge, the efficacy of the divine will, and the wisdom of the divine arrangement that devises sufficient ways to obtain an effect." And because these things neither are "repugnant to the contingency" of the actions nor undermine the in-tegrity of the human actor, the human's agency is not violated.[6]

This kind of thinking forms the background of the claim that God does not violate the integrity of human beings when he speaks through them. Rather, God partners with them by acting in and through their

[3]Thomas Aquinas, *Compendium of Theology*, trans. Richard J. Regan (New York: Oxford University Press, 2009), 103.
[4]Ibid., 106.
[5]Ibid., 103.
[6]Ibid., 109.

unique personalities and historical context to bring about his divine plan. As Scott Swain puts it: "The Spirit who created the human mind and personality does not destroy the human mind and personality when he summons them to his service. Far from it. The Spirit sets that mind and personality free from its blindness and slavery to sin so that it may become a truly free, thoughtful, and self-conscious witness to all that God is for us in Christ."[7] That God sets the human free in this way is an act of grace, one that brings his human partners more into line with his overall will for their lives. "By the grace of God I am what I am," Paul says, "and his grace toward me has not been in vain" (1 Cor 15:10). God uses his chosen people, equipped by the circumstances of the entire order of creation and history that God himself has directed, to speak on God's behalf in accordance with God's will, so that their words are his own divine speech (2 Pet 3:2).

GOD AND WRITTEN WORDS

God relates to the texts that his people produce in much the same way that he does to their human authors. We find a helpful illustration of God's relationship to written words in the stories surrounding Israel's ark of the covenant.[8] God commands Moses to build the ark and place the tablets he would receive on Mount Sinai inside it (Ex 25:10-22). Inscribed on these tablets are the words of the covenant, "written with the finger of God" (Ex 31:18). God then uses the ark as the means by which he relates to and communicates with his people. "There I will meet with you, and from above the mercy seat, from between the two cherubim that are on the ark of the covenant, I will deliver to you all my commands for the Israelites" (Ex 25:22). Here we see a tangible example of how God relates to his chosen texts: he elects to identify his own divine presence with them so that their words can serve a means by which he encounters and relates to his people.

The idea that God would work through written texts makes sense both

---

[7]Swain, *Trinity, Revelation and Reading*, 67.
[8]For this illustration, see Timothy Ward, *Words of Life: Scripture as the Living and Active Word of God* (Downers Grove, IL: InterVarsity Press, 2009), 29-30.

practically and theologically. On a practical level, these texts perma-
nently record and transmit the knowledge of God's words and deeds so
that this knowledge is not lost from one generation to the next.[9] God
reflects this intention when he tells the people to write down his words
so that they and their children "may hear and learn to fear the LORD your
God" (Deut 31:13). His purpose is to work within the limitations of his
finite creatures by giving them a way to pass on their knowledge from
one person to another. The written record also serves as a constant reminder of what God has done. The psalmist reflects on the need for such
a reminder when he recalls God's commandment that the people of
Israel should "teach . . . their children" about what God had done so that
they will "set their hope in God, and not forget the works of God, but
keep his commandments" (Ps 78:5-7). Peter does the same thing when
he notes that he writes his letters "so that after my departure you may be
able at any time to recall these things" (2 Pet 1:14-15).

On another level, however, the composition and transmission of the
texts of Scripture serve a deeper theological purpose. By their very existence, these texts merge God's diverse and particular acts of grace from
across salvation history into a single story so that we are better able to
see how all of God's actions fit within God's divine plan. This purpose is
manifested when God uses the faithful actions of the biblical authors
from the past as the means by which our own faithfulness is prompted
in the present. Peter makes this connection when he explains how his
readers' salvation in Christ stems from words the prophets wrote long
before. "Concerning this salvation," he says, "the prophets who proph-
esied of the grace that was to be yours made careful search and inquiry.
. . . It was revealed to them that they were serving not themselves but you,
in regard to the things that have now been announced to you through
those who brought you good news by the Holy Spirit sent from heaven"
(1 Pet 1:10, 12). Peter's point is that his readers' salvation—which occurs
as God brings about his will for their lives through their hearing of the
gospel—takes place in the way it does in part because of what the

---

[9]On this point, I am following the lead of Swain, *Trinity, Revelation and Reading*, 52-58.

prophets wrote centuries earlier. So God's movement of grace in the past, and the biblical authors' obedient response to it, reverberates here and now as God uses the authors' past actions to produce our faith and obedience in the present. In this way, Scripture itself ties God's various saving acts together to form a single story, a unified history of God's grace and our response to it.

Jesus makes these kinds of connections when he identifies the words of Scripture with God's presence and power in his life. We see this early on when he describes his life as a fulfillment of biblical prophecies (Lk 4:18-21), and again later when he says that the Scriptures "testify on my behalf" (Jn 5:39). He also believes that his words carry authority because, like the words of Scripture, his words are identified with God's presence and action. "Very truly, I tell you," Jesus says, "anyone who hears my word and believes him who sent me has eternal life, and does not come under judgment, but has passed from death to life" (Jn 5:24). And, in the same way God identifies himself with his words of his chosen people Israel, Jesus identifies himself with the words of his disciples: "whoever listens to you listens to me, and whoever rejects you rejects me" (Lk 10:16). He draws out the logic of this connection while praying to the Father in Gethsemane: "the words that you gave to me I have given to them, and they have received them and know in truth that I came from you" (Jn 17:8). Taken together, these claims indicate that when the disciples preach about Christ, they are proclaiming God's own Word. And as they make this proclamation, Christ is present in their words so that their listeners' response to them is a response to Christ himself.

The apostles adopt a similar approach to the relationship between their words and Christ. For example, Peter defends the veracity of his preaching by grounding it in the authority of Christ. "For we did not follow cleverly devised myths when we made known to you the power and coming of our Lord Jesus Christ," he says, "but we had been eyewitnesses of his majesty." And what Peter saw in Jesus was the revelation of God: "For he received honor and glory from God the Father when that voice was conveyed to him by the Majestic Glory, saying, 'This is my Son, my Beloved, with whom I am well pleased.' We ourselves heard this voice come from heaven, while we were with him on the holy mountain" (2 Pet 1:16-18). The connection Peter draws here is significant. God the Father confirmed that Jesus was the revelation of God by audibly declaring him to be his Son. This declaration was heard by his disciples, giving them the ability to confirm that it was true. Peter then links the content of what he heard about Jesus to the content of Old Testament Scriptures: "So we have the prophetic message more fully confirmed" (2 Pet 1:19). In other words, on the basis of God's truthfulness and the consistency of his actions over time, Peter argues that we can read the prophets to learn more about Christ; and likewise, understanding the truth of Christ will help us grasp the true message of the prophets. A direct line runs from the words of Israel's prophets through Christ to Peter's own testimony about him. These distinct words correspond to one another because they all come from same source: the prophets spoke the words of God, and Peter heard the words of this same God proclaimed over Jesus, who himself is the incarnate God of whom Peter testifies with his own words.

Paul makes similar connections when he talks about Christ's life and mission taking place "in accordance with the scriptures" (1 Cor 15:3). By "scriptures" he means the Old Testament, which he says was "written for our instruction, so that by steadfastness and by the encouragement of the scriptures we might have hope" (Rom 15:4). His conviction is that because God has fulfilled his covenantal promises through Jesus, the preaching of the gospel about Jesus should correspond to what the Old Testament teaches. This same conviction is operative when Philip instructs the Ethiopian eunuch struggling to interpret a passage from Isaiah. His method is to start with the Old Testament text and then clarify its meaning in light of Christ: "Philip began to speak, and starting with this scripture, he proclaimed to him the good news about Jesus" (Acts 8:35). The same pattern shows up again and again throughout the New Testament: the apostles appeal to the authority of Old Testament texts and then show how these texts are fulfilled in Jesus. This approach links the authority of their preaching about Jesus to the authority of the Old Testament and thus to God himself. Although the apostles' words are human words, they carry God's power because God speaks in and through them in the same way that he spoke through the prophets and Christ. Or, as Paul puts it, "God is making his appeal through us" (2 Cor 5:20).

In the same way, Peter defends the authority of the apostles' words by grounding their words in the authority of the prophets. "I am trying to arouse your sincere intention," he tells his readers, "by reminding you that you should remember the words spoken in the past by the holy prophets, and the commandment of the Lord and Savior spoken through your apostles" (2 Pet 3:1-2). The context of this statement is a conflict over false teachers in the church, some of whom were instructing the people of the church to return to their former way of life, mostly likely related to keeping the Jewish law (2 Pet 2:20-22). Their claims created a crisis of authority. Whom should the people trust: these teachers, or Peter and the other apostles? By linking his teaching directly to Jesus and the Scriptures, Peter is solidifying his authority as a trustworthy source. The church can know that he speaks the truth because what he speaks lines up with the words of both Scripture and Christ. And not only do Peter's words carry authority, but the words of the other apostles, including Paul, do as well. "So also our beloved brother Paul wrote to you," Peter says, "according to the wisdom given to him, speaking of this as he does in all his letters. There are some things in them hard to understand, which the ignorant and unstable twist to their own destruction, as they do the other scriptures" (2 Pet 3:15-16). Note how Peter links Paul's texts directly to the "other scriptures," implying that they carry the same authority. His texts carry the same authority as the Old Testament because they both have their origin in God, are identified with God's presence and manifest God's power.

CHRIST AND SCRIPTURE

In light of these kinds of connections, Christians talk about God's relationship with the words of Scripture in terms of *inspiration*. Our everyday use of this word in English can be misleading. For example, we might refer to someone as "inspired" when he or she is moved to do something unusual or extraordinary, such as when a sprinter runs an inspired race or an actor gives an inspired performance. However, it would be a mistake to apply the same meaning to Scripture, as if talking about the inspiration of Scripture indicates that God helped the authors write at an especially high level.[10] As true as this may be, the inspiration of Scripture is more about the nature of the text than the abilities of the authors. The theological use of the word has its roots in Paul's claim that "all scripture is inspired by God and is useful for teaching, for reproof, for correction, and for training in righteousness" (2 Tim 3:16). The Greek word for "inspired by God" is *theopneustos*, which can be translated literally as "God-breathed." We use the term "inspiration" to indicate that the words of the Scripture are "breathed out" by God so that they come to us as God's own words. The image is that just as we literally breathe out our words to others to communicate the content of our minds to them, so the words of Scripture are breathed out by God and reflect his own divine wisdom and will.

A key implication of this idea is that Scripture is trustworthy and true in all its claims. This conclusion is based on the nature of God's relationship to the text. Because the words of the Bible come from God and stand in line with his divine will, they reflect God's own qualities and character. Among other things, the Bible says that God "never lies" (Tit 1:2). By extension, we apply this same affirmation to God's Word: it never lies. This corresponds to the understanding of key figures in the Bible, including Jesus and the apostles, who never express doubt about Scripture's claims but always assume their accuracy. Another implication has to do with our interpretation of Scripture. To say that the words of Scripture are God-breathed is to say they must be interpreted in light of Christ because the God who speaks these words is one and the same as the God who became incarnate in Jesus. Because God always acts in a manner consistent with his eternal being and will, anything God says in any part of Scripture will correspond to what he has said and done in Christ for us and for our salvation.

This interpretive principle holds true for the words of the Old Tes-

---

[10]For a development of this point, see Ward, *Words of Life*, 79-84.

The Word of God

tament as well as the New Testament. Even though the texts of the Old Testament were composed centuries before Christ was born, we read them rightly when we interpret them in light of Christ's life, death and resurrection. The same God who spoke through the prophets of ancient Israel acted in the "fullness of time" to gather the entire history of Israel in Christ and bring it to its fulfillment (Eph 1:10). As a result, everything God prompted the Old Testament authors to write corresponds to what God knew he later would say and do in Christ and his Spirit. This reality does not undermine the Old Testament texts, as if it makes them a more basic or primitive revelation from God that should be discarded in light of the fuller revelation God gives us. Instead, it makes these texts theologically and practically relevant to the whole of our lives. Not only does it mean that the God revealed in the Old Testament is the same God revealed in Jesus Christ, but also it means that the Old Testament can be used to instruct us about Christ and our life of discipleship to him. This is Paul's point when he appeals to inspiration to argue that the Scriptures—by which he means the texts of the Old Testament—are "useful for teaching, for reproof, for correction, and for training in righteousness" (2 Tim 3:16). His point is that the entire Old Testament directs us to Jesus because, in God's providence, he intended that these words would serve this precise function when he originally spoke them through the ancient writers.

This idea seems impossible only if we view Scripture strictly as a human text constrained within the limits of a linear, creaturely history. But if we affirm that God speaks in and through Scripture within the context of his one divine plan for history, then we can approach Scripture in light of God's possibilities rather than our own.[11] After all, every created thing exists within the context of God's will for its existence. God does not exercise his will in a random or reactionary way but according to his perfect wisdom and plan. The events narrated in Scripture and the texts themselves are no exception. Each event happened within the context of God's eternal plan, and the biblical writers who recorded these

[11]See Matthew Levering, *Participatory Biblical Exegesis: A Theology of Biblical Interpretation* (Notre Dame, IN: University of Notre Dame Press, 2008), 3-7.

events lived and moved and had their being in the God who was speaking through them. As the very Word of God himself, the eternal Son was actively involved in every part of this history and the lives of the writers. When this same Son came to us in the flesh of Jesus Christ (Jn 1:14), he showed us more clearly what he had been working toward all along. To interpret the words of these writers in distinction from Christ is to misunderstand them, because it is to fail to recognize how and why they were written in the first place. These texts, as Robert Jenson argues, are "a product of Christ's own testimony to his own character, given by the mouth of his prophet." As such, we can and must interpret them in light of him. We can "find out about the historical Jesus Christ from Isaiah or Zechariah or David, and about what Isaiah or Zechariah really meant from Jesus' teaching and story."[12] The entire Bible can be read as a single whole, because one and the same God, the God revealed in Jesus Christ, speaks through all of its words.

TEST CASE: JESUS AND THE PHARISEES

Jesus approaches Scripture in this way during a particularly intense debate with the Pharisees recorded in John 8. This debate is important for our purposes because it unveils key insights about the relationship between Scripture and Christ that will inform our account of the practice of theology. The debate starts with the Pharisees criticizing Jesus. Disturbed by the content of his teaching, they argue that Jesus does not have the authority to make his claims. "You are testifying on your own behalf," they insist. "Your testimony is not valid" (Jn 8:13). This argument stems from the premise that claims about God must be grounded in a trusted authority in order to be considered true. The Pharisees deny that Jesus' claims carry this kind of authority because they do not correspond to their understanding of God based on their own interpretation of Scripture.

Jesus responds by placing his claims in their eternal context. "Even if I testify on my own behalf, my testimony is valid because I know where I have come from and where I am going, but you do not know where I

---

[12]Robert W. Jenson, "Scripture's Authority in the Church," in *The Art of Reading Scripture*, ed. Ellen F. Davis and Richard B. Hays (Grand Rapids: Eerdmans, 2003), 35.

come from or where I am going. You judge by human standards" (Jn 8:14-15). Note how Jesus reframes the Pharisees' conception of authority. Jesus claims to have authority because *he* is the authority on which all such claims can be grounded. This is the point of his statement about his coming and going. He is the eternal Son of God sent by the Father to complete his saving mission and then return to the Father as the risen Lord. All reality and history find meaning and purpose in his mission, and so his life is the criterion by which all claims about God's authority must be measured. No claim about God, his covenant with Israel or the meaning of Scripture can contradict Jesus' teachings because he is one and the same as the God who performed these actions and speaks through the Scripture.

Jesus drives this point home. "In your law, it is written that the testimony of two witnesses is valid. I testify on my own behalf, and the Father who sent me testifies on my behalf" (Jn 8:17-18). Here Jesus is claiming divine identity. He is saying that the Pharisees fail to recognize his authority because they judge him by human standards and do not realize that he is the Son of God who reveals the Father through his words and actions. "You know neither me nor my Father," Jesus says. "If you knew me, you would know my Father also" (Jn 8:19). No further witness to Christ's authority is needed.

As the exchange continues, the Pharisees shift their argument. They do so in response to Jesus' claim that "if you continue in my word, you are truly my disciples; and you will know the truth, and the truth will make you free" (Jn 8:31-32). They reject the link between Jesus' word and the truth of God, and so they call into question his understanding of salvation history. "We are descendants of Abraham and have never been slaves to anyone," they say. "What do you mean by saying, 'You will be made free'?" (Jn 8:33). Their purpose in posing this question is to show that Jesus' claims do not align with Scripture. After all, the people of Israel based their identity on God's promise to Abraham that his descendants would be God's chosen people if they would keep the covenant and the law (Gen 17:1-6). By identifying themselves with Abraham, the Pharisees are claiming this promise as their own possession. They are the religious leaders of Israel, and so they are the ones who have the authority to determine who does and does not stand in line with it. Jesus' words contradict Scripture's account of this promise, they believe, because he insists that a right standing with God comes through following *his* words rather than with the keeping of the law associated with God's promise to Abraham.

The Pharisees here are engaging Jesus in a high-stakes theological debate about the relationship between God and Scripture. They both agree that Scripture is God's Word, and they agree that anyone who speaks the truth about God will make claims that correspond to the claims of Scripture. Yet they starkly disagree about whether Jesus' words correspond to Scripture because they have very different ways of interpreting the biblical text.

On one side, the Pharisees insist that they stand with the truth of God because they alone are rightly interpreting Scripture's account of God's promises to Israel. Jesus cannot be speaking the truth, they argue, because his claim that God's salvation comes through *him* contradicts God's promise to Abraham that salvation would come through his descendants and the keeping of the law. If God acts consistently over time, then what God said to Abraham will match what God says and does in the present. Because Jesus' words contradict God's earlier promises to Abraham, his claims must be untrue. In fact, the only way to believe that Jesus is telling the truth is to reject Scripture's account of God's promises. But this would call both God's character and Scripture into question. If Scripture is God's Word, the Pharisees insist, then Jesus cannot be speaking the truth. He must be a false teacher.

On the other side, Jesus holds firm by insisting that he both speaks the truth about God and fulfills God's promise. He supports his claim and rejects the Pharisees' argument by reconfiguring their understanding of God and his plan for salvation history. "I know that you are descendants of Abraham," he tells them. "Yet you look for an opportunity to kill me, because there is no place for you in my word. I declare what I have seen in the Father's presence. . . . If God were your Father, you would love me, for I came from God and now I am here. I did not come on my own, but he sent me" (Jn 8:37-38, 42). Once again, Jesus outflanks the Pharisees: he grants that they are the biological descendants of Abraham, but he denies this means that they are the heirs to God's promise to Abraham. The problem is that their misguided interpretation of this promise has kept them from recognizing that Jesus himself is the one who fulfills it. This is the mirror image of the Pharisees' argument. Whereas the Pharisees had argued that it is impossible to believe Jesus' words while also believing the scriptural account of God's promise to Abraham, Jesus insists that it is impossible to believe Scripture without also believing *his* words, because he was sent directly by God the Father to bring about what God promised to Abraham long ago. Then he drives his point home: "Whoever is from God hears the words of God. The reason you do not hear them is that you are not from God" (Jn 8:47).

The Pharisees do not take this charge lightly. They accuse Jesus of being a Samaritan—in other words, not truly Jewish—and insist he is possessed by a demon. Jesus responds: "I do not have a demon, but I honor my Father and you dishonor me. Yet I do not seek my own glory; there is one who seeks it and he is the judge. Very truly, I tell you, whoever keeps my word will never see death" (Jn 8:49-51). Here again, Jesus claims that he stands in line with God the Father and that his words are the key to salvation. The Pharisees respond by once again questioning whether Jesus stands in line with God's promises to Abraham. "Now we know that you have a demon. Abraham died, and so did the prophets; yet you say, 'Whoever keeps my word will never taste death.' Are you greater than our father Abraham, who died? The prophets also died. Who do you claim to be?" (Jn 8:52-53). Their point is that Jesus' claims are true only if *he* is more central to God's plan of salvation than Abraham and the prophets. This would seem, in their mind, to contradict everything recorded in Scripture about God's promises to Abraham, Moses, David and every other spiritual leader in the history of Israel. The implication of their question is clear: Jesus could be right in what he is saying only if the whole of Israel's Scriptures are false.

By now we can see that Jesus and the Pharisees are interpreting Scripture differently because they are starting from very different places.

The Pharisees begin their interpretation of Scripture by starting with Abraham. Because the story of salvation begins with God's promise to Abraham, any saving action that God performs in history must be understood in light of this promise and conform to it. Jesus, by contrast, starts with himself. The story of salvation begins with God's choice to save humans through him, and everything that happened before or after his coming into history must be interpreted in light of him. These two starting points give them very different readings of the exact same texts. The Pharisees are reading Scripture through the lens of created history, from Abraham to the present; Jesus is reading Scripture through the lens of divine history, from eternity to eternity.

Jesus' eternal starting point is reflected in his answer to the Pharisees' question: yes, he is greater than Abraham. This is not a boastful claim, he says, but simply the truth. "If I glorify myself, my glory is nothing. It is my Father who glorifies me, he of whom you say, 'He is our God,' though you do not know him. But I know him; if I would say that I do not know him, I would be a liar like you. But I do know him and I keep his word" (Jn 8:54-55). This is a strong claim. Jesus is declaring that he is the key to God's plan of salvation, and as such, everything God promised to Abraham and the other leaders in Israel should be understood in light of *him*. Indeed, Jesus tells the Pharisees, "Your ancestor Abraham rejoiced that he would see my day; he saw it and was glad" (Jn 8:56).

The Pharisees respond to this claim with mocking incredulity. "You are not yet fifty years old, and have you seen Abraham?" Jesus answers with the most dramatic claim yet: "Very truly, I tell you, before Abraham was, I am" (Jn 8:57-58). The implications of this claim are profound, as his listeners would have immediately recognized. By using the phrase "I am" in this manner, Jesus is drawing a direct connection between his own identity and the identity of Yahweh, the God of Israel. Working in the background is the story in which Yahweh gives his name to Moses by saying, "I AM WHO I AM." After giving this name, Yahweh then sends Moses to tell Israel that "I AM has sent me to you" (Ex 3:14). The implication is that Moses' words and deeds carry authority because God himself has sent Moses to speak on his behalf. By using these same words—"I am"—and by saying that he preexisted even Abraham, Jesus is identifying himself directly with God and claiming God's authority as his own. The implication is that no interpretation of Scripture that contradicts Jesus' claims can be true, because *Jesus himself* is the source of every word in Scripture.

Jesus' exchange with the Pharisees—especially his arguments about the relationship between his own actions and works and the being of God—puts us in position to understand how Scripture fits into God's eternal plan for history. If what Jesus says in this passage is true, then every word in Scripture serves Christ's saving mission because he is one and the same as the God who speaks these words. Because we know God as he unites us to Christ by faith through the power of his Spirit—and because this union involves our partnership with God as we follow Christ within the context of his ongoing work within God's plan—we will read and interpret Scripture rightly only when we do so together with Christ himself. He stands at the center of Scripture and is the key to its interpretation. As such, he is the agent who, though the power of his Spirit, deploys Scripture to fulfill its intended purpose within God's eternal plan.

READING WITH CHRIST

We can grasp how Christ uses Scripture in this way—and how our reading of Scripture connects directly to our practice of theology—by looking at a brief episode in John 2.[13] Immediately after Jesus drives the money changers out of the temple in Jerusalem, the people ask him to explain his actions. He responds by saying, "Destroy this temple, and in three days I will raise it up." The people are not sure how to interpret this claim, and they respond with skepticism: "This temple has been under construction for forty-six years, and will you raise it up in three days?" The disciples also are confused by Jesus' answer, at least initially. Yet John adds this explanatory remark: "But he was speaking of the temple of his body. After he was raised from the dead, his disciples remembered that

---

[13]This example is drawn from Richard Hays, "Reading Scripture in Light of the Resurrection," in *The Art of Reading Scripture*, ed. Ellen F. Davis and Richard B. Hays (Grand Rapids: Eerdmans, 2003), 221-24.

he had said this; and they believed the scripture and the word that Jesus had spoken" (Jn 2:19-22). Note how John says that the disciples recognized the meaning of Jesus' claim only later, after the resurrection, when they received a new perspective that helped them grasp the significance of Jesus' words and how they corresponded to Scripture. What caused the disciples to come to this new understanding? Certain clues show us that it does not come through the disciples' own power, as if they finally were able to put the pieces together and figure out what Jesus had meant. Rather, this understanding came to them through the instruction of Jesus himself.

Peter points us in this direction when he says that Christ appeared to his disciples "who ate and drank with him after he rose from the dead. He commanded us to preach to the people and to testify that he is the one ordained by God as judge of the living and the dead. All the prophets testify about him that everyone who believes in him receives forgiveness of sins through his name" (Acts 10:41-43). In this statement, Peter connects the content of his preaching—including the fact that it corresponds to the teachings of the Old Testament prophets—directly to Christ's presence and instruction. The implication is that Peter and the disciples were able to draw these connections because Christ himself taught them how to do so. This corresponds to Jesus' actions on the road to Emmaus, where he shows the two disciples "the things about himself in all the scriptures" (Lk 24:27). He does the same thing with rest of the disciples later on: "He opened their minds to understand the scriptures" (Lk 24:45). Jesus then tells his disciples to wait in Jerusalem for the gift of his Spirit, who takes up this teaching role by reminding the disciples of Jesus' words and telling them "everything" they need to know to think and speak rightly about him (Jn 14:26).

As fellow disciples of the risen Jesus, we learn how to read Scripture rightly in the same way: the Spirit of Christ teaches us how to understand Scripture. He does so, in part, by giving us a share in the mind of Christ (1 Cor 2:16). This spiritual instruction is one of the primary ways that Christ partners with us in God's plan for history. As we participate in his life by the power of his Spirit, he shapes us by utilizing the same Scriptures that shaped his own thoughts and actions. He uses them, for example, to give us knowledge of who he is and what he has done so that we can understand and imitate him better. He also uses them to help us discern what he is prompting us to think and do at any given moment we partner with him. We know that because Christ always acts consistently over time, everything he might be calling us to say or do will correspond to what he has said and done in the past. This means we can measure whether or not we are following Christ rightly by testing whether or not our words and actions match the depiction of Christ in Scripture.

This fits the pattern employed by the first disciples as they engaged in their respective ministries. They appealed to Scripture as standing in line with Christ's authority, and they read it in the way Christ taught them to read it. As such, it served as the criterion by which they understood Christ's being and character and the standard for their own thinking and speaking about God. The same principle applies to us in our discipleship to Christ, particularly as we practice the discipline of theology. A theologian seeking knowledge of Jesus Christ is going to be a student of Scripture precisely because "Jesus Christ is the same yesterday and today and forever" (Heb 13:8). The risen Jesus we follow and obey today is one and the same as the God who spoke through the prophets, lived and died as the incarnate Son and led his apostles to preach and teach the gospel accurately. Scripture gives us access to all of these moments of his life, and nothing Christ will lead us to think or say in the present will contradict this biblical account. We proceed rightly in theology when we believe both that Scripture leads us to the knowledge of Christ and that Christ is the key to understanding the meaning of Scripture.

This insight helps us recognize one of the important implications of the exchange between Jesus and the Pharisees: it is possible to know Scripture without knowing the God of Scripture. Even though the Pharisees accepted the authority of Scripture and were able to cite passages in support of their positions, they failed to recognize that God was standing right in front of them. They did so because they interpreted the biblical text in distinction from Jesus. By making this error, the Pharisees stand in a long line of people who have encountered Jesus but failed to recognize his identity or the true nature of his mission. Even Christ's own family, those who presumably knew him the best, tried to restrain him from his ministry thinking that he had "gone out of his mind" (Mk 3:21). Knowledge of Scripture—and even knowledge of details about the life of Christ—is not mutually exclusive with spiritual blindness. A right engagement with Scripture and Christ involves more than knowing what Scripture says or knowing the facts about Jesus; we also have to understand what Scripture says and who Jesus is within the broader context of God's eternal plan and our participation in it. This understanding comes as a result of the Spirit's work to enlighten our minds and enable us to think and live in the pattern of Christ himself. He is the one who gives us eyes to see and ears to hear what God is doing so that we can find our place in it. He also is the one who equips us to bring our lives into correspondence with what God is doing.

We shut ourselves off from the Spirit's guidance whenever we approach the text on our own terms, like the Pharisees did when they saw it from the starting point of created history. We can easily fall into the same kind of error as theologians, such as when we ask, "How is this text relevant to my life?" or, "What theological truth can I draw from this passage?" Such questions get things backward. Scripture's purpose is not to help us fit God into our lives but to see how our lives fit into what God is doing in history through Christ and the Spirit. Rather than trying to insert Scripture into our reality by figuring out how we might apply it to our lives, our task is to reinterpret our lives and the whole of reality in light of Scripture.[14] The Bible does not just tell us true historical things; it proclaims the true history, and it does so by directing us to Jesus, the one by whom all history is defined. This means we have to approach the text confessionally as well as academically, with the eyes of faith as well as those of an objective researcher. We see the text not merely as a repository of stories and facts from which we can draw theological information but as a holy instrument through which the living God en-

---

[14]For an insightful analysis of this point, see J. Todd Billings, *The Word of God for the People of God: An Entryway into the Theological Interpretation of Scripture* (Grand Rapids: Eerdmans, 2010), 75-86.

counters us in power and grace. We bring our reason and experience to the text, but we do so as people whose reason and experience are united to Christ and thus subject to being transformed by his Spirit as we live in discipleship to him.

That Scripture would play this role corresponds to God's plan for our lives and for the whole of history. God created us in order to *be* with us, to share his eternal life by making us his children. He maintains this posture even after we sin, refusing to withdraw himself from us or save us from a distance. He instead reaches out to us in our need and comes to us, as Herman Bavinck says, by entering "into the human fabric, into persons and states of being, into forms and usages, into history and life."[15] He does so preeminently in Jesus, and the grace of Christ is manifested in the words of Scripture that testify to him and the Spirit who helps us hear them rightly. This grace corresponds to God's eternal being, and the existence of Scripture is a tangible testimony to him. God does not work over our heads but through our words, making himself present and accessible to us while, at the same time, leading us beyond ourselves into fellowship with Christ in anticipation of the life to come. The fact that he does so gives theologians hope. If God can work through human words in this kind of way, then perhaps he can work through ours as well.

---

[15]Herman Bavink, *Reformed Dogmatics*, vol. 1: *Prolegomena*, trans. John Vriend (Grand Rapids: Baker Academic, 2003), 442-43.

- five -

HEARING THE WORD OF GOD

℘

Near the beginning of *The Confessions*, Augustine reflects on the way he learned how to speak as a child. He notes that this skill did not come through formal instruction but by observing and listening to the people around him. When someone called an object by a name, he remembered that word and used it for that same object. He paid attention when particular facial expressions and tones were linked with certain words and phrases, and he made connections between people's gestures and their sentences. "In this way," he says, "I gradually built up a collection of words, observing them as they were used in their proper places in different sentences and hearing them frequently. I came to understand which things they signified, and by schooling my own mouth to utter them I declared my wishes by using the same signs."[1] In other words, Augustine learned how to speak by hearing the speech of others while living in community with them. He did not repeat everything they said in exactly the same way they said it. Instead, he learned the meaning of their words and adopted their patterns of speech so that he could communicate his own ideas through his own speech.

In a similar way, theologians learn how to speak about God by observing and listening. While we often say new things, we do not say whatever we want. We pay attention to how words and phrases are used

---

[1]Augustine, *The Confessions*, trans. Maria Boulding, O.S.B (Hyde Park, NY: New City Press, 1997), 11.

so that we can learn their proper meaning. Grammar is important to us. We adopt specific rules of speaking so we can communicate clearly while avoiding confusion and misunderstanding. The difference is that, unlike the young Augustine, we are learning to speak about God rather than created realities. Because God is distinct from every creature, we cannot rely solely upon what other people say about him. We have to listen to God's own speech. As theologians, we learn to speak by observing and listening to God as he lives his divine life together with us within the context of salvation history. We do so in community with Jesus Christ and the Holy Spirit as well as with other Christians who also live in and through them.

Scripture plays a central role in this process. As we saw in the previous chapter, the Bible is not merely a repository of facts about God's past deeds that we are called to excavate, investigate and then organize into applicable theological knowledge. It is the chief creaturely instrument through which God speaks. He uses it to reveal himself to us, judge our sin, call us to repentance and propel us into a fuller participation in his life and plan. This participation includes the transformation of our minds and the refinement of our language so that we can think and speak about God correctly. Scripture serves as the instrument by which we refine our ideas and words and measure our usage of them. We think and speak rightly about God when what we say corresponds to what he has spoken in this text.

The challenge, of course, is that the words of Scripture must be interpreted in order to be understood. How do we know that we are interpreting Scripture accurately? What criterion do we use for this interpretation? And how do we sort through different and often divergent readings of the biblical text? This chapter addresses these questions in four sections. The first uses the writings of Augustine to establish the proper framework from which we can measure our interpretation of any given passage of Scripture. The second discusses the implications of the fact that we hear Scripture in community, not only with Christ and the Spirit but also with the church both living and dead. The third uses a particular debate from Paul's letters as a test case to help us see how we might apply a Christ-centered approach to history to our interpretation of the text. And the fourth draws these threads together to present a picture of what it looks like for theologians to hear God's speech in Scripture rightly in partnership with Christ by the power of his Spirit.

READING IN LOVE

Because God employs Scripture within the context of his eternal plan, his use of it will correspond to the saving work that stands at the center of this plan. We will know that we are hearing God's speech in Scripture correctly if our encounter with the biblical text is moving us in the same direction that God is moving us through Christ and the Spirit. But how can we determine whether or not this is happening? Augustine provides a helpful framework from which to make this determination. He argues that we should measure our interpretation of every passage by whether or not this interpretation is prompting us to a deeper love for God and neighbor, because this double love is the defining mark of God's saving work in history.

Augustine grounds this approach on the presupposition our lives are ordered by God's plan to establish a loving relationship with us. God loves us, and he wants us to love him in return. We live in accordance with this love, Augustine thinks, when we enjoy God as our highest good. To enjoy something is "to hold fast to it in love for its own sake."[2] God's will is for us to enjoy him by loving him. Created things are not meant to be enjoyed but used to enrich our love for God: "to use something is to apply whatever it may be to the purpose of obtaining what you love."[3] As long as we order our lives so that we enjoy God and use created things in the service of our love for God, we live in accordance with God's plan.

The problem is that we do exactly the opposite. Due to our sin, we enjoy created things and then use God to justify our pursuit of these things. Augustine thinks this problem has its roots in the fact that God's divine being is "inexpressible" to us, such that we can only think of him

---

[2] Augustine, *On Christian Doctrine* 1.4.4. Quotations from this text are drawn from *Teaching Christianity: De Doctrina Christiana*, trans. Edmund Hill, O.P. (Hyde Park, NY: New City Press, 1996).
[3] Augustine, *On Christian Doctrine* 1.4.4.

based on our "ideas of bodily excellence."[4] This leaves us picturing God
in creaturely terms and producing idolatrous images of him. Our sinful
nature exacerbates this tendency by prompting us to seek fulfillment in
fleeting pleasures and temporary possessions. As a result, our love for
God is "blocked by our love for inferior things."[5] This leaves us with "an
entirely false happiness" and a life that contradicts God's plan.[6]

God responds by reordering our lives through Jesus Christ. As the
true image of God, he replaces our idolatrous images by becoming incarnate in human flesh. Not only does this give us an embodied picture
of God we actually can grasp, but it also provides us an example to imitate. Now, we can know and follow God by focusing on the human Jesus
rather than created things. In this way, Jesus himself becomes the pathway
to our enjoyment of God. Or, as Augustine puts it: even though Jesus
Christ is "actually our homeland"—because he is one and the same as
the God who is our highest good—he becomes "the road to our
homeland."[7] We learn to love God by following Christ in discipleship and
taking the "trek to our homeland" together with him.[8]

Now that Christ has ascended into heaven, Augustine believes God
uses Scripture to bring order to our lives. Scripture functions much like
Christ's human nature did: it reveals the wisdom of God through accessible human words and prompts us to love God in the pattern of Christ.
We use Scripture rightly when we read it to discover "the thoughts and
will of the authors it was written by, and through them to discover the
will of God, which we believe directed what such human writers had to
say."[9] In other words, Scripture should be seen as God's speech given to
us to help us love him as our highest good. Our challenge is that there
are "problems and ambiguities of many kinds" in the biblical text. Not
only do these ambiguities lead to misunderstandings of the texts, but also

[4]Augustine, On Christian Doctrine 1.6.6–7.7.
[5]Augustine, On Christian Doctrine 1.3.3.
[6]Augustine, The City of God 19.4, in The City of God Against the Pagans, ed. and trans. R. W. Dyson,
    Cambridge Texts in the History of Political Thought (New York: Cambridge University Press,
    1998).
[7]Augustine, On Christian Doctrine 1.11.11.
[8]Augustine, On Christian Doctrine 1.10.10.
[9]Augustine, On Christian Doctrine 2.5.6.

they lead to disagreements regarding how best to interpret it. Augustine insists that these problems do not reflect faults in the text itself—as if God spoke inconsistently or unclearly—but rather, they are part of God's purpose for the text. "I have no doubt that this is all divinely predetermined," he says, "so that pride may be subdued by hard work and intellects which tend to despise things that are easily discovered may be rescued from boredom and reinvigorated."[10] In fact, one of the ways God uses difficult passages is to prompt us to explore other parts of Scripture, because every obscure point in the text can "be found quite plainly expressed somewhere else" in the Bible.[11]

Of all the texts that can bring clarity, Augustine thinks that Matthew 22 is the most important, because it shows us how Jesus himself interpreted Scripture. The passage begins with the Pharisees testing Jesus by asking him, "Teacher, which commandment in the law is the greatest?" Jesus responds to them: "'You shall love the Lord your God with all your heart, and with all your soul, and with all your mind.' This is the greatest and first commandment. And a second is like it: 'You shall love your neighbor as yourself.' On these two commandments hang all the law and the prophets" (Mt 22:36-40). Augustine believes that Christ's quotation of these two commandments stands in line with God's desire that we enjoy him above all creaturely things. After all, when we love God in this way, he says, we do not "leave room for wanting to enjoy something else" as our highest good.[12] The love of God does not detract from the love of neighbor, he argues; instead, it explains precisely how we love our neighbor: "God is to be loved on God's account, and one's neighbor on God's account."[13] He explains that we love our neighbor precisely by loving God above all things, because our love for God bears witness to our neighbor that he or she should love God in the same way. In this way, our neighbor is "swept toward the same destination as that to which the whole flood of our love is directed."[14]

---

[10]Augustine, *On Christian Doctrine* 2.6.7.

[11]Augustine, *On Christian Doctrine* 2.8.

[12]Augustine, *On Christian Doctrine* 1.21.

[13]Augustine, *On Christian Doctrine* 2.10.

[14]Augustine, *On Christian Doctrine* 1.21.

Augustine defends the idea that these two commandments should serve as our lens for interpreting Scripture by appealing to Christ's statement that "all the law and the prophets" hangs on them (Mt 22:40). This reveals that Christ measures his own interpretation of every passage by whether or not it produces love of God and love of neighbor. Augustine argues that we should follow Christ by interpreting Scripture in the same way. We will know that our interpretation of a passage is acceptable when this interpretation prompts us to have a deeper love for God and neighbor. If it does not, then we must be misinterpreting the passage. "So anyone who thinks that he has understood the divine scriptures or any part of them," Augustine says, "but cannot by his understanding build up this double love of God and neighbor, has not yet succeeded in understanding them."[15] From Augustine's perspective, this method corresponds with Paul's description of "faith working through love" (Gal 5:6). We read Scripture through the lens of our faith in Christ when we interpret it in light of God's love. This way of reading accords with the eternal life we will have in Christ as we stand before the Father in love (Eph 1:4).

Augustine's framework for interpreting Scripture is based on the idea that God actively uses our reading and interpretation of Scripture to propel our lives of discipleship to Christ. This idea connects to traditional Christian claims about Scripture's *illumination*. God's relationship to the Bible does not cease once it is written, as if he simply turned the words loose after the human authors wrote them. Rather, God continues to uses these words in new ways over time to bring about his divine will in the lives of his people. That God uses Scripture in this way is a sign of his faithfulness. Long before we were born, God prompted the authors of Scripture to write texts that God knew he would later use in his relationship with us. As Paul puts it: "whatever was written in former days was written for our instruction, so that by steadfastness and by the encouragement of the scriptures we might have hope" (Rom 15:4). God ordered salvation history so that the pathway of our life together with him involves the text of Scripture.

---

[15]Augustine, *On Christian Doctrine* 1.36.40.

Christians appeal to illumination as they affirm that whenever God speaks to us, God also enables our minds to hear, understand and respond to what he says. This fits how Paul works out the implications of the inspiration of Scripture: "All scripture is inspired by God and is useful for teaching, for reproof, for correction, and for training in righteousness, so that everyone who belongs to God may be proficient, equipped for every good work" (2 Tim 3:16-17). The "so that" reveals God's intention: God speaks to us so he can form us into the people he created us to become. He accomplishes this goal by illumining our minds to grasp and then obey his words.

God's act of illumination is associated with the Holy Spirit, because the Spirit's power is linked both to God's speech and to its effectiveness in our lives. For example, as Peter looks back to the history of Israel, he says that the Spirit is the one who called Israel's prophets to their ministry and gave them the words they said to the people: "No prophecy ever came by human will, but men and women moved by the Holy Spirit spoke from God" (2 Pet 1:21). The Spirit works in a similar way in the life of Jesus, who inaugurates his ministry by quoting Isaiah 61:1: "The Spirit of the Lord is upon me, because he has anointed me to bring good news to the poor. He has sent me to proclaim release to the captives and recovery of sight to the blind, to let the oppressed go free, to proclaim the year of the Lord's favor" (Lk 4:18-19). Peter's ministry reflects this pattern when he is filled with the Spirit as he proclaims the gospel to the priests and elders in Jerusalem (Acts 4:8). The same is true for Paul, who preaches the gospel and performs miracles as a testimony to Christ through the power of the Spirit (Acts 13:9). In all of these cases, the Spirit's activity is linked to God's speech, and the goal of the Spirit's action is to use this speech to shape God's people in line with what God has accomplished through Christ. This corresponds to Christ's promise that the Spirit will be the one who will "testify on my behalf" and "take what is mine and declare it to you" (Jn 15:26; 16:14).

The Spirit's illumining testimony is necessary rather than optional for us, because without it, God's action remains beyond our comprehension. Paul picks up on this theme when he describes his preaching as a "demonstration of the Spirit and of power" (1 Cor 2:4). He explains that the gospel seems like foolishness to the natural mind because the Spirit alone can enable us to recognize the truth about God: "no one comprehends what is truly God's except the Spirit of God" (1 Cor 2:11). The Spirit activates God's revelation within us by opening and then enriching our minds to be able to receive and understand it. This explains why God's truth is "veiled to those who are perishing" but unveiled to those who are enabled to see "the light of the gospel of the glory of Christ, who is the image of God" (2 Cor 4:3-4). The Spirit makes all the difference. He helps us interpret Scripture rightly by directing us to Christ and enabling us to work out the implications of Christ's revelation for our understanding of God and our lives together with him. The result is a life of love for God and neighbor that corresponds to the love we will share with God for eternity.

HEARING WITH THE CHURCH

That we need the Spirit's guidance reflects the reality that even though we know Christ, we still face the temptation to think in idolatrous ways because we see the truth of God dimly. Scripture is the Spirit's chosen instrument to help us avoid this temptation. John Calvin uses the analogy of a person with weak eyes who sees rightly only when he wears glasses. Scripture functions in a similar way, he says, by "gathering up the otherwise confused knowledge" in our minds and showing us how to see all things in light of Christ.[16] This clarification does not take place as a one-time event but as an ongoing process as the Spirit refines and remakes us through our repeated engagement with Scripture over the course of our lives. Dietrich Bonhoeffer emphasizes this point when he notes how the first Christians dedicated themselves to the ongoing teaching of the apostles (Acts 2:42). They gave "continuing attention" to this instruction because they realized that they had to be actively learning in order to remain faithful to God's continual action in history.[17]

---

[16]Calvin, *Institutes of the Christian Religion*, 1.6.1.
[17]Dietrich Bonhoeffer, *Discipleship*, Dietrich Bonhoeffer Works, vol. 4, ed. John D. Godsey and Geffrey B. Kelly (Minneapolis: Fortress, 2001), 227.

The same principle holds for us. We should be engaging with Scripture constantly so that the Spirit can use it to shape us more and more into Christ's image. This involves testing everything in our lives to see if it matches what God has revealed (1 Thess 5:21). As we do so, the Spirit prompts us to repent and change as needed so that we can "grow up in every way into him who is the head, into Christ" (Eph 4:15). In this way, Scripture serves as the instrument by which the Spirit shapes us so that we can be more faithful partners with Christ as he continues to work in line with God's saving plan.

As the Spirit personally uses Scripture to speak to us, he also works by bringing us into conversation with other Christians who also are hearing God's speech in Scripture. This corresponds to God's goal for our lives. God does not envision isolated individuals standing before his throne in eternity, but a community. From his promise to bring salvation through Abraham's descendants (Gen 12:1-2), to his declaration that Israel would be his treasured people (Ex 19:3-6), to his announcement that the church exists as "God's own people" (1 Pet 2:9), God has always worked through groups of people in line with his divine plan. We reflect the corporate nature of God's work when we—with our distinct personalities, gifts and abilities—are "activated by one and the same Spirit" and exist as Christ's one body in the world (1 Cor 12:11). And because this same Spirit guides our lives through Scripture, it makes sense that we should read and interpret Scripture in light of the gifts and insights the Spirit has given the church as a whole.

Hebrews provides direction as we consider how we should incorporate the church's insights into our thinking. After explaining the content of God's message regarding his Son, the author warns that "we must pay greater attention to what we have heard, so that we do not drift away from it" (Heb 2:1). The link between these two clauses is instructive. If the act of paying attention to the message keeps us from drifting away from it, then our drifting away from the message is the result of a failure to pay attention. The author then lists three sources who have delivered this message so that we can know to whom we should pay attention. The message, he says, "was declared at first through the Lord, and it was attested to us by those who heard him, while God added his testimony by signs and wonders and various miracles, and by gifts of the Holy Spirit, distributed according to his will" (Heb 2:3-4). The first source is the Lord Jesus; the second is the apostles. God himself is the third source, because he adds direct testimony through his miracles as well as by distributing the gifts of the Spirit. This reference to the gifts of the Spirit directs us to the church, the people of God who have received spiritual gifts according to God's will.

The implication is that, along with Christ and the apostles, we also need to pay attention to the voice of the church in order to avoid drifting away from God's message. This fits the nature of God's saving work. If we believe that God still partners with his people as they live their life in Christ—and if we think the Spirit continues to disperse his gifts to the church—then it makes sense that we should pay attention to the church's voice and consider it a source of accountability for our thinking and speaking about God. This corresponds to Paul's description of the church's "ministry of reconciliation," which he says comes as the result of God's act of "entrusting the message of reconciliation to us" so that we can be "ambassadors for Christ" (2 Cor 5:18-20). God has gifted the church to carry the message of Christ into the world. In light of this gifting, we should listen to what the church has to say. And because the church includes not only the living but also the dead—the believers whose lives and work constitute the great tradition of Christian thought—we should pay attention to this tradition so that we do not drift away from the message of Christ as we interpret Scripture in our own time and place. Over the course of church history, the message of Christ has been linked to the rule of faith, an early summary of Christian beliefs that serves as the foundation for statements like the Apostles' Creed. The content of this rule is traditionally identified both with Jesus' instructions to his disciples about how to read Scripture in light of his saving work (Lk 24:27) and the teaching that apostles like Paul received from Christ and then passed on to the churches (1 Cor 15:1-3). The church's conviction has been that if we read the Bible through the lens of the rule of faith, then we will interpret the text in a way that corresponds to the message delivered by Christ and the apostles.[18]

We will do so, however, knowing that the church itself has no authority to determine the content of God's message. The church is a source to which we should pay attention only because *God* has commissioned it with the task of delivering the message of Christ and gifted it to do so. Our deference to the teaching of the church is thus deference to God's act of entrusting his message to it. And as we give this deference to the voice of the church, we recognize that the church is made up of finite and flawed people like us. While we often think and speak in accordance with God, sometimes we make mistakes because we see things "only in part" (1 Cor 13:9). Other times we turn our back on what God has said and manipulate his divine revelation to serve our own human purposes. The church often does the same thing: it can be wrong in its interpretation of Scripture.

Paul reflects this reality when he chastises the Galatians for turning away from the truth about God. "I am astonished," he tells them, "that you are so quickly deserting the one who called you in the grace of Christ and are turning to a different gospel—not that there is another gospel, but there are some who are confusing you and want to pervert the gospel of Christ" (Gal 1:6-7). The ever-present reality that the church might depart from the truth in this way means that we constantly have to assess the church's claims. Human speech about God has to be measured by the standard of God's own speech, which for us means measuring it by the words of Scripture. As the church, both living and dead, offers us insights about how best to interpret and understand God and his actions, our task is to bring these insights to Scripture and see if what the church says corresponds to the text. We do so trusting that the Spirit works consistently over time. If he has illumined the church and its members with unique insights about how best to interpret Scripture, this illumination will correspond to all of

---

[18]For a helpful treatment of the relationship between the rule of faith and our interpretation of Scripture, see Scott Swain, *Trinity, Revelation and Reading: A Theological Introduction to the Bible and Its Interpretation* (London: T&T Clark, 2011), 106-14.

God's actions through history, including God's speech throughout the whole of Scripture.

The fact that we have to measure constantly the church's teaching by the standard of Scripture is one of the great benefits of listening to the church. As we listen to other Christians, they prompt us to read the Bible again with new questions and insights. We do so knowing that we might end up interpreting the text in new and different ways as a result. If we find that Scripture contradicts what others in the church are saying, however, our task is to bring these insights back to them to question and perhaps correct this faulty teaching. This may mean entering into dialogue or debate with other Christians. This back-and-forth exchange can be mutually enriching as we draw from the insights of others while also teaching them what we know and understand. Sometimes, however, these exchanges can be challenging as we find ourselves disagreeing with others about the meaning of a specific passage or about how to interpret Scripture more generally. These kinds of disagreements are to be expected given the fact that God calls a church made up of finite and fallen people. It is inevitable that some members will not hear and understand his revelation in Scripture rightly or completely.

Such disagreements also might reflect the nature of God's working out of his good plan for creation. Because God does not bring about his goals all at once but gradually and in "the fullness of time" (Gal 4:4), God's work often takes place in different ways as history progresses. Every age and culture is distinct. As God's saving plan continues to unfold, Christ acts in new and fresh ways to bring about God's will through his Spirit. While these actions will correspond to everything he has done in the past—because God acts consistently and Jesus Christ himself is "the same yesterday and today and forever" (Heb 13:8)—they may not be identical to what God has done in the past. Richard Bauckham makes this point when he says that God "may act in new and surprising ways in which he proves to be the same God, consistent with his known identity, but in unexpected ways. He is both free and faithful. He is not capricious, but nor is he predictable. He may be trusted to be consistent with himself, but he may surprise in the ways he proves consistent with himself."[19] For example, even though God's saving work in Christ was consistent with his prior actions and promises to Israel, this work was still surprising and new. Jews who came to faith in Christ did not have to throw out everything they had believed, but they did have to change and adapt their prior thinking about God in order remain faithful to what God had shown them in Jesus. They did so by turning back to Scripture and seeing that, in fact, Christ's actions stood in line with God's promises even though they did so in ways no one anticipated.

As we hear Scripture in conversation with the church, we should assume that the one unchanging God continues to work in new and surprising ways today. The Spirit helps us recognize the new ways God is working by using these events to prompt us to return to Scripture and read it again with new eyes. This process is one of the key ways the Spirit continues to reform and renew the church. For instance, God may equip certain members to call the church to repent or change in light of God's present work. When we hear this kind of call, our task is to return to Scripture, seek clarity from the text and then respond. Sometimes, we accept the message and repent. Other times, we push back against the criticism. We do so knowing that we are members of "one body and one Spirit" with all the church's members even when we disagree with them. We engage our critics "with all humility and gentleness, with patience, bearing with one another in love, making every effort to maintain the unity of the Spirit in the bond of peace" (Eph 4:2-4). As with any such activity, debates may arise as the church sorts out what is true and how to respond. Such debates are not signs of weakness but of strength. The Spirit often uses our disagreements to prompt us to grow as individuals while at the same time prompting "the body's growth in building itself up in love" (Eph 4:15-16). In fact, theological debates often serve as the context in which we learn how to interpret Scripture correctly in light of our double love for God and neighbor—especially the neighbor with whom we disagree.

---

[19]Richard Bauckham, *Jesus and the God of Israel: God Crucified and Other Studies on the New Testament's Christology of Divine Identity* (Grand Rapids: Eerdmans, 2008), 53.

TEST CASE: CIRCUMCISION

Paul's participation in the early church debate about Gentile circumcision provides us with an example of how a theological disagreement can help us learn how to read and interpret Scripture faithfully. This debate may seem odd to the modern reader, but it was important enough to the early church that it shows up in several of Paul's letters and throughout the book of Acts. For our purposes, it serves as a good test case for seeing the implications of interpreting Scripture in light of God's plan to unite us to himself in love through Christ and the Spirit.

On one side of the debate is a group of Christians known as the Judaizers.[20] They have this title because they insisted that Gentile converts to Christianity adopt Jewish practices like circumcision and the keeping of the law after coming to faith in Christ. They defended their position by appealing to Scripture, and particularly to God's promises about Israel's role in God's plan of salvation. Jesus was not just anyone, they argued— he was the Messiah of Israel, the one who had come to restore God's chosen people and fulfill the promises God had made to them. The people of Israel were the biological descendants of Abraham, the one to whom God had made the promise that "in you all the families of the earth shall be blessed" (Gen 12:3). God chose Abraham's heirs to be the people through whom he would save all nations. For the Judaizers, this choice carried a clear implication: the Gentiles' faith in Christ is just the starting point for their salvation because it gives them entrance into God's covenant with Israel. Once inside the covenant, however, they have to keep the covenant. The first step toward doing so is the act of circumcision. God had established this act as the special sign of the covenant, telling Abraham that anyone who was not circumcised "shall be cut off from his people" (Gen 17:14). Once they were circumcised, they then needed to obey the commandments of the law, because God said "cursed be anyone who does not uphold the words of this law by observing them" (Deut 27:26).

---

[20]This description of Paul's opponents is drawn from Bruce W. Longenecker, *The Triumph of Abraham's God: The Transformation of Identity in Galatians* (Edinburgh: T&T Clark, 1998), 25-34.

From the Judaizers' perspective, the requirement that the Gentiles be circumcised and keep the law stands directly in line with the teaching of Scripture. After all, God keeps his promises. If it were possible for the Gentiles to be saved through their faith in Israel's Messiah without having to be circumcised and keep the law, then God's promises to Israel and his warnings about disobeying the law would be null and void. But that cannot be if Scripture is true. How could God turn his back on the promises and commandments he had given to Israel? Doing so would call into question either God's integrity and character, on the one hand, or the truthfulness of Scripture, on the other. Because neither option is acceptable, the Judaizers believe the proper conclusion is obvious. If God's promises and commandments to Israel are trustworthy, and if the Scriptures are true, then the Gentiles who come to faith in Christ also must be circumcised and keep the law.

Paul strongly rejects the Judaizers' position, and he develops his rationale for doing so throughout his letters. Interestingly, he builds his case from many of their same premises, because he likewise affirms the truthfulness of Scripture and insists that God has not turned his back on the promises or the law. He also agrees that the Gentiles' salvation cannot be separated from God's covenant with Israel, as if their faith in Jesus could be detached from the history of Israel in some way. Despite this common ground, however, Paul thinks his opponents have misinterpreted Scripture because they have made one key mistake: they have tried to understand Christ in light of Israel instead of understanding Israel in light of Christ.

This interpretive mistake stems from an improper approach to reality and history. Paul believes that we cannot view history on creaturely terms, as if the movement of time in a linear, moment-by-moment fashion defines the nature of the reality into which God and his will must fit. Rather, we have to see history in light of the fact that creation itself exists according to God's eternal plan for it. God revealed this plan most fully in Jesus Christ, and this revelation gives us the ability to understand what God has been doing in history all along. The Judaizers misunderstand this revelation because they are thinking about God in a human way, leaving them blind to how the Gentiles fit into God's plan and his promises. Paul thinks that if they reframed the direction of their thinking, they could see that God has been acting in a consistent and faithful way throughout Israel's history to the present.

These assumptions prompt Paul to offer a Christological interpretation of reality, history and Scripture as a counterargument to the Judaizers' position. This interpretation is grounded on his foundational beliefs that God "chose us in Christ before the foundation of the world to be holy and blameless before him in love" and that God "has made known to us the mystery of his will, according to his good pleasure that he set forth in Christ, as a plan for the fullness of time, to gather up all things in him, things in heaven and things on earth" (Eph 1:4, 9-10). Paul thinks that God always had planned for Christ to stand at the very center of history. He also believes that God always had intended for Christ's life, death and resurrection to serve as the climax of Israel's story. This Christ-centered perspective on Israel elevates rather than diminishes Israel's role, because now the true nature of God's plan for Israel has been unveiled: they were chosen as God's people because they were to be the people of Christ. From before the foundation of the world, God ordered history around his plan to save both Jews and Gentiles through their faith in Jesus rather than their obedience to the law.

This approach to reality and history leads Paul to interpret God's promises to Abraham and his commandments about circumcision and the law in a Christ-centered way. On each topic, he reconfigures the Judaizers' interpretation of Scripture by starting with Jesus and then reinterpreting it in light of the saving work of Christ and the Spirit's work in the life of the Gentiles.[21]

With respect to Abraham, Paul reframes the Judaizers' understanding of God's promise by asking his opponents a question: Was Abraham put in right standing with God before or after he was circumcised? Clearly, it was before Abraham was circumcised, because God counted him

---

[21]Paul's arguments along these lines are worked out in more depth in Richard B. Hays, *Echoes of Scripture in the Letters of Paul* (New Haven, CT: Yale University Press, 1989), 84-121. My treatment of these themes is indebted to this work.

righteous because of his faith rather than his circumcision (Rom 4:10-11). On the basis of this claim, Paul argues, Abraham's true descendants—the people who have been granted the same kind of right relationship with God that Abraham himself had—are not his biological heirs but those who share the same kind of faith he had (Rom 4:11-25; Gal 3:6-9). God's intention all along was to fulfill his promise to Abraham by leading his people to faith (Gal 3:16), and now we can see what God truly meant when he promised that Abraham would be the "ancestor of a multitude of nations" (Gen 17:5-8). This promise was never meant to be fulfilled by Abraham's biological descendants but by the people who come to faith in Christ: "there is no longer Jew or Greek . . . for all of you are one in Christ Jesus. And if you belong to Christ, then you are Abraham's offspring, heirs according to the promise" (Gal 3:28-29).[22] So God has kept his promise, but he has done so unexpectedly, in a broader and richer way than anyone imagined, by keeping it through Jesus. And Scripture is true—and so is the work of the Spirit in the Gentiles—as long as we interpret them both in light of a Christ-centered view of God's plan in history.

Paul applies the same line of reasoning to circumcision. He questions the idea that a physical act like circumcision can make someone a member of Israel and instead points to passages that refer to a circumcision of the heart (Deut 10:16; 30:6; Jer 4:4). God never intended the act of circumcision to be merely "something external and physical," he argues, but rather something "spiritual and not literal" (Rom 2:28-29). This reflects God's eternal plan: our communion with God does not happen on the basis of our obedient actions but through our inner transformation that enables us to share in his divine love. This kind of transformation happens only through grace, and the good news is that God has given believers this grace through Christ and the Spirit. "But when the fullness of time had come," Paul explains, "God sent his Son, born of a woman, born under the law, in order to redeem those who were under

---

[22]For a fuller exploration of this insight, see Richard R. Hays, "Abraham as Father of Jews and Gentiles," in *The Conversion of Imagination: Paul as Interpreter of Israel's Scripture* (Grand Rapids: Eerdmans, 2005), 61-84.

the law, so that we might receive adoption as children. And because you are children, God has sent the Spirit of his Son into our hearts, crying, 'Abba! Father!' So you are no longer a slave but a child, and if a child then also an heir, through God" (Gal 4:4-7). The true heirs of God's covenant promises are not those who are physically circumcised, therefore, but those who have been redeemed by Christ and indwelled by his Spirit as a result of their faith. This stands in line with God's original plan to "justify the circumcised on the ground of faith and the uncircumcised through that same faith" (Rom 3:30). In other words, through their faith in Christ and the gift of the Spirit, both Jews and Gentiles can experience the circumcision of the heart that God always intended to accomplish even if they never are physically circumcised. Again, God has kept his promise and the Scripture is true, but both of these things can be seen for what they are only in light of Jesus.

This insight connects directly to Paul's approach to the law. In light of Christ, he argues, the verse "cursed be anyone who does not uphold the words of this law by observing them" (Deut 27:26) does not mean that Gentiles have to obey the law in order to be saved, as the Judaizers claim. Rather, it demonstrates the futility of the law, because it shows that "all who rely on the works of the law are under a curse" (Gal 3:10). The good news is that Jesus took the burden of this curse on himself so that his people would not have to bear it. "Christ redeemed us from the curse of the law by becoming a curse for us—for it is written, 'Cursed is everyone who hangs on a tree'—in order that in Christ Jesus the blessing of Abraham might come to the Gentiles, so that we might receive the promise of the Spirit through faith" (Gal 3:13-14). Through his death on the cross, Christ redirected the curse for Israel's disobedience onto himself. This act not only means that the Gentiles can be saved but also inaugurates a new age in which both Jews and Gentiles can receive the Spirit who enables them to obey God more faithfully than they could have under the law. In this sense, Paul thinks, God's act in Christ and the Spirit does not cancel out the law but fulfills it. "For God has done what the law, weakened by the flesh, could not do: by sending his own Son in the likeness of sinful flesh, and to deal with sin, he condemned sin in the flesh, so that the just requirement of the law might be fulfilled in us, who walk not according to the flesh but according to the Spirit" (Rom 8:3-4). After all, God's original purpose for the law was for his people to live righteously, and so the true members of his people are not those who still keep the law but those who have their righteousness in Christ by the Spirit. So, once again, Paul thinks that God's original intentions have been accomplished: "Christ has become a servant of the circumcised on behalf of the truth of God in order that he might confirm the promises given to the patriarchs, and in order that the Gentiles might glorify God for his mercy" (Rom 15:8-9).

It is important to see the pattern at work in Paul's arguments here. He reconfigures the Judaizers' understanding of Abraham, circumcision and the law by arguing in each case that God's saving work in Christ and the Spirit sheds new light on the meaning of God's original promises recorded in Scripture. His method is to ask, "Now that we see God's salvation of both Jews and Gentiles through their faith in Jesus Christ, what must God's promises to Israel have really meant?" He then reads Scripture in light of this question and concludes that salvation through Christ was always God's plan and that those united to Christ by the Spirit do not need to be circumcised or keep the law to be Abraham's heirs.

This pattern is reflected in Paul's conclusion that the "the revelation of the mystery that was kept secret for long ages but is now disclosed, and through the prophetic writings is made known to all the Gentiles, according to the command of the eternal God, to bring about the obedience of faith" (Rom 16:25-26). Note the connection Paul draws between Scripture—"through the prophetic writings"—and God's work in the Gentiles. The fact that Jesus Christ would be the one to bring about God's plan remained a mystery until he accomplished it. But now that Christ has come, God uses the biblical texts composed before Christ—texts composed within the context of God's covenant with Israel—to make Christ known to the Gentiles and to prompt their lives of faith and obedience. And all of this is "according to the command of the eternal God" in the fulfillment of his saving plan for history.

It is crucial to recognize the key point of difference between the Judaizers' approach and the one Paul employs. Even though they both are trying to make a theological judgment about how God's covenant with Israel relates to God's act of salvation in Jesus Christ, Paul does so by using Christ as the lens through which to view history, while the Judaizers do so by using history as the lens through which to view Christ. This difference explains their divergent interpretations of Scripture. Paul frames his interpretation of Israel's covenant in light of how God fulfills it in Christ, while the Judaizers frame their interpretation of Christ in light of what believers must do in obedience to the covenant. Paul thinks the Judaizers' approach is a mistake because it causes them to turn their gaze away from God and onto themselves. This shift leads them to try to "make a good showing in the flesh" and convince others to be circumcised "so that they may boast" about them (Gal 6:12-13). As a result, they effectively "nullify the grace of God" and act as if "Christ died for nothing" (Gal 2:21). In contrast, Paul continually shifts his gaze away from himself toward Christ: "may I never boast of anything except the cross of our Lord Jesus Christ, by which the world has been crucified to me, and I to the world" (Gal 6:14). Paul sees this Christ-centered approach as the pathway to freedom (Gal 5:1), and he believes it results in the fruit of the Spirit, which is a life that reflects God's intentions for the covenant all along (Gal 5:22-23).

THEOLOGY OF THE WORD

Paul's debate with the Judaizers informs our work as theologians by leading us to a key insight: we approach Scripture rightly when we view the whole of created reality and history, and every part of the biblical text, through the lens of God's saving plan in Christ and the Spirit. This divine plan continues to unfold even now. As the risen and ascended Lord, Jesus continues to work in line with God's plan as he intercedes for us before the throne of the Father (Rom 8:34). He performs this work, in part, by partnering with us as we follow him in discipleship. This involves his acts of calling and equipping us through Scripture and then helping us understand it through the illuminating power of his Spirit. The Spirit "helps us in our weakness" by interceding for us when do not know what to think or say (Rom 8:26-27). He gives us the right words so we can serve as Christ's ambassadors as we proclaim the gospel to the world (2 Cor 5:20). Along the way he enables us to "live in a manner worthy of the gospel" by leading us to love God and neighbor in the pattern of Christ's love (Phil 1:27). We do so by living sacrificially, putting the interests of others before our own. In this way, we begin to live in obedience to Paul's commandment that we should become "imitators of God, as beloved children, and live in love, as Christ loved us" (Eph 5:1-2). This life of sacrificial, self-giving love marks our participation in the life of God in anticipation of our eternal future together with him.

This is the context in which we approach Scripture as theologians. Our calling is to help the church think and speak about God correctly so the church can partner with Christ in God's saving plan for history, and we interpret the biblical text in light of this calling. Our primary goal is not to extract isolated doctrinal truths from the text and then use them as the building blocks of a theological system. Our goal is to help the church interpret Scripture faithfully so that the church can follow Christ as the Spirit leads. This means we interpret each passage in light of how Christ and the Spirit are prompting us to live in relation to God and neighbor right now. Because their work in history is ongoing, our interpretation of Scripture takes place as an ongoing process of discernment. We return to the text constantly in light of what the Spirit is doing so we might hear what he is calling us to think, say and do in partnership with Jesus.

We engage in this task knowing the text will be interpreted properly only in light of the *living* Christ. As he continues to act in history, we have to keep listening to what he is calling us to do along with him. The Spirit gives us the ability to hear Christ's call by enlightening our minds so that we understand what he is saying. Because the Spirit uses Scripture for this purpose, our proper response is to read it with humility, openness and the expectation that God might surprise us. We cannot approach Scripture by "folding our arms and adopting the stance of onlookers or spectators," Karl Barth says. Instead, "the only possibility is that of seriousness, of decision, of being taken captive, of faithfulness, of an active and supreme spontaneity."[23] The chief way we develop this kind of posture is to be held accountable to Scripture's claims while also paying attention to the Spirit's illumining work in the lives of other believers. For example, when Paul wrote to the Galatians who were influenced by the Judaizers' argument, he asked them to pay attention to what the Spirit was doing in and through the church. "Having started with the Spirit, are you now ending with the flesh? Did you experience so much for nothing?—if it really was for nothing. Well then, does God supply you with the Spirit and work miracles among you by your doing the works of the law, or by your believing what you heard?" (Gal 3:3-5). Paul's point here is to direct his readers to the Spirit's presence and work in their lives and implore them to view Scripture and history in light of it. "If we live by the Spirit," Paul insists, "let us also be guided by the Spirit" (Gal 5:25).

We see this approach at work in Acts 15 when the church in Jerusalem makes theological decisions in response to the circumcision debate. The scene begins in Antioch when some Christians take the Judaizers' line that the Gentiles have to be circumcised to be saved. Paul and Barnabas, of course, strongly disagree with this claim, and after "no small dissension and debate" (Acts 15:2), the church in Antioch sends the parties to Jerusalem to seek the wisdom of the apostles and elders in the church there. Yet they also are divided on the question, and again there is "much debate" about the issue (Acts 15:7). At a pivotal point, however, Peter rises and begins to talk about his own ministry among the Gentiles. "God, who knows the human heart, testified to [the Gentiles] by giving them the Holy Spirit, just as he did to us," he says, "and in cleansing their hearts by faith he has made no distinction between them and us. Now therefore why are you putting God to the test by placing on the neck of the disciples a yoke that neither our ancestors nor we have been able to bear? On the contrary, we believe that we will be saved through the grace of the Lord Jesus, just as they will." Paul and Barnabas then speak and recount "all the signs and wonders that God had done through them among the Gentiles" (Acts 15:8-12).

[23]Karl Barth, *The Göttingen Dogmatics: Instruction in the Christian Religion*, vol. 1, trans. Geoffrey W. Bromiley (Grand Rapids: Eerdmans, 1991), 254.

After their speech, the apostle James, the leader of the church in Jerusalem, begins to speak. After noting that God has clearly been working among the Gentiles, he verifies that this work stands in line with Scripture: "This agrees with the words of the prophets." He cites a passage from Amos about God restoring "even all the Gentiles" to a right standing with him (Acts 15:16-17; Amos 9:11-12), and he then draws his conclusion. On the basis of the Spirit's ongoing work and the authority of Scripture, the Gentiles do not need to be circumcised in order to be faithful to Christ. After his speech, and with "the consent of the whole church" (Acts 15:22), the apostles and elders send a delegation to Antioch with Paul and Barnabas to deliver a letter saying that "it has seemed good to the Holy Spirit and to us" not to require that the Gentiles be circumcised. Instead, they should abstain from food and immoral practices that might lead Jewish Christians to break table fellowship with them (Acts 15:28-29).

Note how the church in Jerusalem came to its theological judgment. In the midst of stark disagreements about how best to interpret Scripture, the turning point happened when Peter talked about how the Spirit was working in the lives of the Gentiles to bring them to faith in Christ. This testimony, along the supporting evidence of Paul and Barnabas, prompted James and the rest of the church to turn to Scripture and see if the work of the Spirit in the Gentiles corresponded to what Scripture says about God's promises and actions. Once they determined that this present work corresponded to the biblical text, they embraced this work and reconfigured their understanding of God, Christ and the practices of the church in light of it. So, in short: they started with the work of Christ and the Spirit, looked to Scripture to help them make sense of these divine actions and then determined how best to participate in these actions in light of what Scripture revealed. In doing so, they grew closer to Christ, came to a fuller knowledge of his grace and lived more in line God's eternal love in their relation to God and others.

This example serves as a template for how we should engage the biblical text as theologians. As we interpret Scripture, our goal should be to adhere to the subject matter to which the church bears witness: God as he has

encountered us in and through the saving history of Jesus Christ and the
Holy Spirit. Paul's life testifies to the faithfulness of this approach. As a
former Pharisee and persecutor of Christians, he had once understood the
biblical passages about God's covenant with Abraham, circumcision and
the law in much the same way as the Judaizers. His interpretations of these
passages changed after he became a Christian because he realized that
these promises and commands must be seen in the light of Christ and the
ongoing work of his Spirit. This premise forms the substance of his opposition to the Judaizers. Their mistake was not that they were incom-
petent interpreters of the Bible but that they interpreted it in light of their
assumption that they were at the center of God's plan for history rather
than Christ. Paul's arguments against their position can be read as a call to
be humble enough to revise their views about God and themselves in light
of what God had revealed. From his perspective, created reality and human
history should not be understood as the context into which Christ enters
as much as the space and the place contextualized by him, because Christ
reveals God to us more clearly and thus extends the limits of what we could
otherwise know. "The gospel that was proclaimed by me is not of human
origin," Paul says, "for I did not receive it from a human source, nor was I
taught it, but I received it through a revelation of Jesus Christ" (Gal 1:11-12).

To be a theologian is to begin our thinking and speaking about God
from this same starting point. We learn how to speak not by listening to
words of human origin but by listening to the words of God. He speaks
to us in Scripture, and we hear him within the context of what he is doing
in our lives through Christ and the Spirit. We offer our interpretation of
what we have heard to the church to help it learn how to speak about God
better than before. We do so by placing our insights alongside those of
the rest of the church, building on what the entire church has heard and
adding our own voices to its ongoing conversation about how best to
partner with God in his saving work. We trust that God will use our
theological work to further his plan for history. To proceed in this way—
measuring our words about God by Scripture in community with the
church within the context of God's saving plan in Christ and the Spirit—
is what it looks like to practice theology while living as a disciple of Jesus.

- six -

THE MIND OF CHRIST

℗

The preceding chapters have provided a framework for the practice of theology built on our confession of faith in Jesus Christ. This framework shows that theology has its origins in God's decision to unite himself to us so that we might share in his eternal love. He created us in his image and likeness so that we might know and partner with him in the working out of this plan. We sought to live on our own terms, however, and the result was a broken relationship with God, darkened minds and death. But because God loves us, he saved us. He sent his Son to unite himself to us and his Spirit to indwell us so that, through them, we could be redeemed from our sin and live eternally as adopted children of the Father. This saving work makes us creaturely participants in God's life, and this participation happens in the present as we grow in the knowledge of God and live in conformity to God's will. We do these things by living as disciples of Jesus Christ by the power of his Spirit. Our life of discipleship begins when we come to faith in Christ, and it continues as we partner with Christ by working together with him within the context of God's eternal plan.

As theologians, we pay special attention to the fact that our partnership with Christ includes our act of taking "every thought captive to obey Christ" (2 Cor 10:5). Even though we have no choice but to use human words to think and speak about God, we seek to use these words in such a way that our ideas and speech correspond to the truth of God.

The incarnate Jesus serves as the standard by which we measure the meaning of our words, and he helps us figure out how to bring our language into conformity to God by speaking to us in Scripture. He also sends his Spirit to illumine our minds so we can hear and understand his speech. The Spirit does this work both directly and by leading us to listen to the voice of the church, made up of both the living and dead.

Now we come to a new question: What do theologians who practice theology within the context of their participation in God through Christ and the Spirit look like? In other words, if we practice theology from the starting point of our faith in Jesus, what kinds of qualities and characteristics will we display? How will we go about our work? And what will be our goals? This chapter and the next seek to address these questions. This chapter focuses on the nature of our theological practice by looking at the life of Jesus Christ. This starting point makes sense given the fact that we know God only as the Spirit gives us a share in Christ's mind within the context of our life of discipleship to him. If we want to understand the nature of our theological knowledge, then we need to understand Christ's mind and how we relate to it. Even though our participation in Christ's mind is not identical to the formal practice of theology, this participation serves as the ground of our theological work and the field in which it takes place. And because our participation in Christ occurs as we live in discipleship to him, our theological work can be better understood when we see it in relation to the practices central to this life of discipleship. When we see our work through this lens, we discover that the practice of theology is one of the ways we obey Paul's command to be "transformed by the renewing of your minds, so that you may discern what is the will of God" (Rom 12:2).

This argument develops in three stages. We begin by looking at Paul's depiction of "the mind of Christ" in order to discern the qualities and characteristics we should display as we participate in it. Then, we look to Jesus to see how he expressed his theological knowledge of God through his actions and practices. The chapter closes with an account of theological practice that follows from our participation in the mind of Christ.

THE PATTERN OF CHRIST'S MIND

Paul develops the theme of the "mind of Christ" in two key passages: Philippians 2 and 1 Corinthians 2. In both passages, he argues that Christ's mind is revealed through acts of self-sacrificial humility performed out of love. He also shows that as we participate in Christ's mind through the power of his Spirit, we will be prompted to act in this same way.

In Philippians 2, Paul deploys his description of Christ's mind in order to illustrate the kinds of qualities and actions that a church living "in a manner worthy of the gospel of Christ" will display (Phil 1:27). His central argument is that a church will live in line with the gospel when its members share *koinonia* with one another through the Spirit (Phil 2:1). As we saw in a previous chapter, *koinonia* can be translated as "fellowship," "partnership," "communion" or "sharing." Paul uses this word when he wants to describe people who live in union with one another even as they remain distinct. Here he argues that the church lives in *koinonia* when its members act out of humility and a desire to serve. "Make my joy complete," Paul says. "Be of the same mind, having the same love, being in full accord and of one mind. Do nothing from selfish ambition or vain conceit, but in humility regard others as better then yourselves. Let each of you look not to your own interests, but to the interests of others" (Phil 2:2-4).

It is at this point that Paul, in order to give an illustration of a life marked by this kind of selfless humility, turns to the example of Jesus Christ.

> Let the same mind be in you that was in Christ Jesus,
>
> who, though he was in the form of God,
>> did not regard equality with God
>> as something to be exploited,
> but emptied himself,
>> taking the form of a slave,
>> being born in human likeness.
> And being found in human form,
>> he humbled himself

and became obedient to the point of death—
even death on a cross.

Therefore God also highly exalted him
and gave him the name
that is above every name,
so that at the name of Jesus
every knee should bend,
in heaven and on earth and under the earth,
and every tongue should confess
that Jesus Christ is Lord,
to the glory of God the Father. (Phil 2:5-11)

In this passage, Paul connects Christ's mind to his status and actions. Christ has the same status as God. He has the "form of God," shares God's name—"the name that is above every name"—and is exalted and worshiped as "Lord." But Christ displays his divine status in an unexpected way. He does not claim its privileges or exploit it to his own advantage. Instead, he empties himself and takes the form of a slave by taking on human flesh. Then, during the course of his human life, he continues this self-sacrificial pattern of action by humbling himself in obedience even to the point of his death on the cross.

The key to interpreting this passage is to understand the connection between Christ's identity as God and his acts of humility and obedience. As Michael Gorman points out, this connection can be interpreted in two starkly different ways.[1] The first way interprets Christ's acts of emptying and humbling himself as *contradicting* his identity as God. This approach sees the phrase "though he was in the form of God" as indicating that acts of humility and obedience are out of character for God. After all, God is the creator and sustainer of all things, and he rules over creation as its sovereign and powerful Lord. He is above his creatures, not below them. So when Christ performs acts of humility and obe-

---

[1]See Michael Gorman, *Inhabiting the Cruciform God: Kenosis, Justification and Theosis in Paul's Narrative Soteriology* (Grand Rapids: Eerdmans, 2009), 25-29. My treatment of this passage is shaped by the exegesis found in this work as well as Gorman's *Cruciformity: Paul's Narrative Spirituality of the Cross* (Grand Rapids: Eerdmans, 2001).

dience during his incarnate life, he is acting in a human rather than a divine way. Christ's resurrection and exaltation mark his return to his proper status as the one who stands high above all people and things. This kind of interpreter might paraphrase the passage in the following way: "Although Jesus has the status of God—and, by his very nature, God cannot humble himself in obedience like a human slave—Jesus contradicted his status by acting in humility and obedience during his human life and death on the cross. But God later elevated Christ back to his rightful place so that everyone now can recognize his true status as Lord."

In contrast, the second way of interpreting this passage sees Christ's acts of emptying and humbling himself as *embodying* his identity as God. This approach emphasizes that Christ's acts of humility and obedience reveal God's true being and thus overturn our mistaken expectations about the nature of divinity. God confirms that Christ's actions are an expression of his divine nature by exalting the humble and obedient Jesus as Lord. An interpreter of this sort might offer the following paraphrase: "Although Jesus has the status of God—and thus people expected that he never would humble himself in obedience like a human slave—Jesus confounded their expectations by humbly taking the form of a slave during his human life and death on the cross. God verifies that the humble and obedient Christ revealed the truth about his divine being by giving him the title Lord. Now everyone can see and know what God is truly like."

The best way to assess these two interpretations is to work out their respective implications. The first interpretation is problematic because it commits us to saying that Christ does not truly reveal God through his actions either in his preexistent eternal state (when he empties himself) or during the course of his incarnate life (when he humbles himself in obedience). This stands in tension with the biblical claims that Christ makes God known to us (Jn 1:14-18), that he is the revelation of "the power of God and the wisdom of God" (1 Cor 1:24) and that "in Christ God was reconciling the world to himself" (2 Cor 5:19). How could Christ reveal God's power and wisdom—and how could God himself be acting through Christ to save the world—if Christ's actions stand in contradiction to God's true being and character?

The second interpretation is stronger, because it works from the assumption that Christ acts in a consistent way throughout his entire life and that his actions correspond to his divine being and character. His pre-incarnate decision to empty himself and become human does not contrast with but expresses his divine character; his obedience and self-sacrifice during his life are a revelation of his eternal divine being; and his exaltation is not the result of a "promotion" to a new position, or a return to a position he had surrendered, but a declaration of his true identity as God.[2] When Christ acts humbly and gives himself sacrificially in love, he is not contradicting his divine being but revealing it. He is showing us the heart of God. This fits with the idea that we will eternally worship a sovereign Lord who was crucified, the "Lamb that was slaughtered" (Rev 5:12). The true God must be seen not only as the all-powerful ruler over all things but also as the sovereign Lord who humbled himself in obedience to the point of death because of his great love for us.[3]

Jesus reflects this picture of God when he says that any persons wanting to be his disciples will need to "deny themselves and take up their cross daily and follow me" (Lk 9:23). His point is that the life of discipleship to him should be marked by the same kind of self-denial and self-sacrifice that marks his own life. "Whoever wishes to become great among you must be your servant," he instructs his followers, "and whoever wishes to be first among you must be slave of all." And Jesus makes it clear that these kinds of instructions are not merely for us—as if he intends to live in a different way—but rather, they conform to his own way of being: "For the Son of Man came not to be served but to serve, and to give his life a ransom for many" (Mk 10:43-44). By presenting the image of this same Christ to the Philippians, Paul gives them a concrete picture of what it means to live like the Jesus they proclaim in the gospel message. A church living in a manner worthy of the gospel

[2]See Gorman, *Inhabiting the Cruciform God*, 30.
[3]See Richard Bauckham, *Jesus and the God of Israel: God Crucified and Other Studies on the New Testament's Christology of Divine Identity* (Grand Rapids: Eerdmans, 2008), 45.

will be one whose members live in mutual self-sacrifice before one another in the pattern of Christ. They will be known not for their high
status or ability to wield power but for their acts of humility and service.
The members will place the needs of other people before their own, and
they will do so out genuine love for one another.

This passage stands in line with Paul's depiction of the Christian life
throughout his letters. For example, after he tells the Galatians that Christ
has freed them from sin by uniting himself to them, he instructs them
about how to use their new freedom. "For you were called to freedom,
brothers and sisters; only do not use your freedom as an opportunity for
self-indulgence, but through love become slaves to one another" (Gal
5:13). Paradoxically, the freedom of the Christian is marked by a willingness to serve others sacrificially in love. We cannot muster this kind
of selflessness on our own, Paul says, but only as the Spirit empowers us
to imitate Christ rather than "gratify the desires of the flesh" (Gal 5:16).
Those "guided by the Spirit" are not "conceited, competing against one
another, envying one another," but instead display "a spirit of gentleness"
and a willingness to "bear one another's burdens" in the pattern of Christ
(Gal 5:25–6:2). He makes this same argument to the Ephesians when he
hints that a life marked by self-giving love not only reflects the example
of Christ but also corresponds to God's eternal plan for our lives. "Be
imitators of God," he says, "as beloved children, and live in love, as Christ
loved us and gave himself up for us, a fragrant offering and sacrifice to
God" (Eph 5:1-2). The phrase "beloved children" calls to mind Paul's description of God's eternal plan to adopt us as his children earlier in the
letter (Eph 1:5), and this connection helps us to see how this pattern of
life relates to our salvation. A person who imitates Christ's humility and
sacrifice lives in the image and likeness of the triune God, who himself
lives an eternal life of mutual self-giving love as Father, Son and Spirit.
We see this life displayed as the Father gives everything to the Son (Jn
16:15), the Son glorifies the Father (Jn 14:13) and the Spirit gives glory to
the Son (Jn 16:14). God makes us participants in this life when the Father
sends the Son to unite himself to us and the Spirit pours God's love into
our hearts so that we can love others (Rom 5:5; 1 Jn 4:12). As we imitate

Christ's humility and service, we bear the image of the triune God in the world; and as we do so in community with others, we live in a way that anticipates our eternal future.

These insights bring us to 1 Corinthians 2, where Paul explains how God enables us to participate in the mind of Christ. He begins by telling the Corinthians that he did not use "lofty words" in his preaching to them but instead directed them to the crucified Jesus (1 Cor 2:1-2). He came "in weakness and in fear and in much trembling" because he did not want them to be persuaded through "plausible words of wisdom" but by "the power of God" (1 Cor 2:3-5). Paul's goal here is to demonstrate that his posture reflects the content of the gospel. He embodies the same kind of humility Christ displayed as he preaches so that his method matches the content of his message. This posture does not reflect his lack of confidence in his words but his trust that God will work powerfully through them.

God exercises this power in a way that corresponds to the content of his eternal wisdom, which comes not as "a wisdom of this age" but as "God's wisdom, secret and hidden, which God decreed before the ages for our glory" (1 Cor 2:6-7). The fact that God would reveal his divine wisdom through Christ's crucifixion is surprising, Paul says, to the point that no one could have conceived of it in advance (1 Cor 2:8-9). Acts of humility, weakness and self-sacrifice contradict our mental picture of how God reigns as the sovereign ruler of all things. But this picture often reflects our own fallen and finite perceptions of divinity. The nature of God cannot be judged by the standards of our own human wisdom, because God's being is beyond what we can imagine. We must be told and shown what God is truly like if we are going to think and speak about God correctly. And Paul thinks that if we begin with what God has said and done, our thinking and speaking about God will focus on the crucified Jesus Christ.

The unexpected nature of this revelation explains why it can be understood only "through the Spirit; . . . [who] searches everything, even the depths of God" (1 Cor 2:10). The Spirit enables us to think about God rightly by helping us "understand the gifts bestowed on us" in Christ; and he empowers us to speak rightly about God so we can explain "spiritual things to those who are spiritual" (1 Cor 2:12-13). While our thoughts and speech may seem foolish to the world, this is because God's wisdom can only be "spiritually discerned" (1 Cor 2:14). Our claims about God are "subject to no one else's scrutiny," Paul says, as if they first need to be verified by the standards of human reason before they can be counted as true (1 Cor 2:15). We base our claims about God on his revelation in Christ, and the Spirit helps us understand what this revelation means by making us participants in "the mind of Christ" (1 Cor 2:16). This participation is the ground of our theological claims: we know the truth about God because we share in the very wisdom of God.

Paul's argument in this passage complements his claims in Philippians 2 by showing us that we acquire the mind of Christ only as the Spirit joins us to Christ by grace. Paul's posture as he talks about God shows us that our possession of this knowledge goes together with the same kind of humility, weakness and self-sacrifice Christ displayed during this life. As such, it cuts against the grain of our fallen nature. The way of the world is to lift ourselves up above others and to seek our own advantage. But God's ways are not like our ways, and our knowledge of God follows suit. When God comes to us in Jesus, he shows us the truth about his divine being and then gives us the ability to think and live in correspondence to it so that we can bear his image and serve as his ambassadors. He does so that we might bear witness to him by loving the world with the same kind of sacrificial love with which God himself loves.

Bringing the content of these two passages together gives us a clearer sense of what it looks like to think and speak faithfully about God as theologians. We know God rightly when we know Christ, and we acquire this knowledge as we live together with Christ by the Spirit. Because life with Christ is characterized by acts of humility and sacrificial love, we come to know God within the context of a life marked by these kinds of actions. We bear witness to our knowledge of God when we live in humility before others; and we use our knowledge rightly when we deploy it not for our own benefit but for the benefit of the people around us out of love for them. And because Jesus continues to work in history for the sake of his people, we practice theology rightly when we use our work for this same purpose in partnership with him. It is in this way that our pursuit of the knowledge of God merges with our discipleship to Christ.

IMITATING CHRIST

We can acquire a clearer picture of the actions that correspond to our participation in the mind of Christ by looking at the practices and activities Christ engaged in as he reflected on God over the course of his incarnate life. Doing so will help us understand how our theological knowledge relates to the rest of our Christian life, because it will give us a practical description of how someone who truly knows God lives and acts.

A helpful text for this purpose is John's account of the Passover meal that Jesus shared with his disciples on the night before his crucifixion.[4] To set the context for this meal, John lets the reader know that the results of Jesus' ministry in Jerusalem have been mixed. While some people believe in him, most do not; and many who believe are keeping their faith secret out of fear of the religious authorities who oppose Jesus (Jn 12:37-43). In light of this situation, Jesus offers a final proclamation about the content of his message and the consequences at stake. "Whoever believes in me," he says, "believes not in me but in him who sent me. And whoever sees me sees him who sent me. . . . I have not spoken on my own, but the Father who sent me has himself given me a commandment about what to say and what to speak. And I know that his commandment is eternal life. What I speak, therefore, I speak just as the Father has told me" (Jn 12:44-45, 49-50). Here Jesus draws a direct link between the Father and himself, because he wants his listeners to understand that his words and deeds are a revelation of God's being and his plan for history. This plan leads to eternal life, and anyone who follows Jesus will obtain eternal life through him. There is much at stake in how someone responds to his words.

After this pronouncement, the scene shifts to the upper room where

---

[4]The interpretation of the passage offered here has been drawn, in part, from the insights of Thomas Goodwin, *The Heart of Christ* (Carlisle, PA: Banner of Truth Trust, 2011), 4-28.

Jesus and his disciples have gathered for the Last Supper. John frames the moment by taking the voice of an omniscient narrator so that he can describe Jesus' internal reflections about his own life and mission from God. "Now before the festival of the Passover, Jesus knew that his hour had come to depart from this world and go to the Father. Having loved his own who were in the world, he loved them to the end" (Jn 13:1). Jesus is aware that his human life is coming to its conclusion, and in line with his saving mission, his thoughts turn toward the people he loves and came to save. John chooses his words carefully to communicate the depth of Jesus' thoughts and feelings at this moment. The phrase "his own" indicates that the people Jesus loves are not just objects or things to him. The people Jesus loves are "his own" in the sense of being intimately part of him, "members of his body" (Eph 5:30). The phrase "to the end" indicates something that is reaching its perfection or completion. In the context of Jesus' reflections on his saving mission, this phrase indicates that Jesus' love for his disciples will continue into eternity, to its perfection and fulfillment through their eternal participation in God's love as his children. It will do so precisely because of what Jesus will do through his coming death and resurrection.[5]

With these specific thoughts in mind, Jesus acts. "And during supper Jesus, knowing that the Father had given all things into his hands, and that he had come from God and was going to God, got up from the table, took off his outer robe, and tied a towel around himself. Then he poured water into a basin and began to wash his disciples' feet and wipe them with the towel that was tied around him" (Jn 13:2-5). This story has become so familiar that the shocking nature of Jesus' act may be lost on us. During the time in which Jesus lived, the roads were unpaved and sometimes served as sewers and dumpsters.[6] Most people's sandal-clad feet were filthy and unsanitary, and foot washing was a necessary task. The act often took place around mealtime, especially when guests were involved. One of the

---

[5] See Ibid, 7-8.
[6] The historical insights offered here are drawn from Richard Bauckham, *The Testimony of the Beloved Disciple: Narrative, History and Theology in the Gospel of John* (Grand Rapids: Baker Academic, 2007), 192-93.

most basic signs of respect and hospitality was to give one's guests a basin and towel so they could wash their feet. And if the host was wealthy enough to have slaves, he would show respect for his guests by having the slaves perform this task. The host himself—or anyone who had high status and standing—would never perform this task. "In a society highly conscious of relative status," Richard Bauckham explains, "it would be unthinkable for this uniquely servile act to be performed for an inferior by a superior in the social scale" because such an act would be an "incomprehensible contradiction of their social relationship."[7] But this is precisely what Jesus does for his disciples. As they prepare for the Passover meal, Jesus—their teacher, the Messiah, the Son of God—humiliates himself by taking the form of a slave and washing their feet.

John carefully frames this event so that his readers recognize that Jesus' act stands directly in line with his knowledge that "the Father had given all things into his hands, and that he had come from God and was going to God" (Jn 13:3). That all things were in Jesus' hands is a reference to his status as the sovereign Lord. It indicates that he holds a position above every other power and authority and that no one has a higher status than he does. Jesus' knowledge that he had come from God and was going to God is a reference to his own saving mission as the eternal Son. To reflect on the fact that he had "come from God" is to think about his decision to become a human being, to empty himself in order to join his life to ours and save us from sin. To reflect on the fact that he is "going to God" is to think about the eternal life he will live before the Father in the Spirit. Jesus knows that he will live this life with us, because we exist in union with him. And so Jesus is thinking here not only about his own status as God but also about the specific way he has chosen to use his status: he has used it to save us by coming to us so that he might unite us to God. It is in the context of these precise thoughts—with his own eternal life and saving mission on his mind—that Jesus washes his disciples' feet. By linking these thoughts and this action together, John wants us to see that Jesus' decision to wash his disciples' feet is not out of character for Jesus.

[7]Ibid., 193.

Rather, this act expresses his divine being and his will for our lives. When Jesus sets aside his status and humiliates himself before his disciples, he is revealing the true nature of God and the depth of God's love for us.

The shocking nature of Jesus' act is reflected by the question Peter asks when Jesus comes to him. "Lord, are you going to wash my feet?" (Jn 13:6). Peter is not oblivious, as if he cannot see what Jesus is doing. He just does not understand why Jesus would do it. Peter knows that Jesus is the Messiah, the long-awaited king of Israel, the one whom God will use to bring salvation to the world. He has confessed that Jesus is the "Son of the living God" (Mt 16:16). Why would someone with this high status act like a slave? It does not make sense. Jesus answers: "You do not know now what I am doing, but later you will understand." But Peter responds by telling him, "You will never wash my feet." Jesus answers, "Unless I wash you, you have no share with me." Peter responds in exasperation: "Lord, not my feet only but also my hands and my head!" And Jesus responds, "One who has bathed does not need to wash, except for the feet, but is entirely clean" (Jn 13:7-10).

This exchange is fascinating on many levels, but the likely thought processes working behind both Peter's response and Jesus' reply are particularly instructive. Peter rejects the foot washing not to be stubborn but because he believes that this act contradicts Jesus' status as Lord. He is convinced that Jesus has sovereign power over all things and can bring redemption to the world. From his perspective, Jesus' decision to act like a slave is tantamount to undermining his own identity and mission. But Peter misunderstands both of these things. If Jesus Christ is truly God, as Peter confesses, then everything Jesus does corresponds to God's being and will. As Karl Barth puts it: "who God is and what it is to be divine is something we have to learn where God has revealed himself . . . and if he has revealed himself in Jesus Christ as the God who does this, it is not for us to be wiser than he and to say that it is in contradiction to the divine essence."[8] In this case, Christ reveals God to be a God who acts in humility to serve others out of love.

---

[8] Karl Barth, *Church Dogmatics* IV/1 (Edinburgh: T&T Clark, 1957), 186.

Why does Jesus display his humility through this particular act? Jesus'
somewhat cryptic response gives us a clue. When he tells Peter that the
only way he can have a share with him is to be washed by him, Jesus is
not saying that Peter literally has to have his feet washed in order to be
saved. He is saying that this act of foot washing is the interpretive key to
unlocking the meaning of Jesus' life and mission. What Peter fails to
grasp is that everything Jesus has done during his incarnate life—from
the moment he emptied himself to be born of Mary until his death on
the cross in front of her and the mocking crowds—expresses the same
kind of humility and self-sacrifice he demonstrates at the feet of his disciples. There is no other way to salvation: the God who has the power to
save is the God who exercises this power through the humility and obedience of Christ to bring about our salvation. Any approach to God that
rules out what Christ reveals, as if God could not do things like this because they contradict his divine status, misunderstands the true nature
of God's being and our salvation.

This insight leads us to Jesus' explanation of the implications of his
act to his disciples. After he returns to the table, Jesus asks them, "Do
you know what I have done to you? You call me Teacher and Lord—and
you are right, for that is what I am. So if I, your Lord and Teacher, have
washed your feet, you also ought to wash one another's feet. For I have
set you an example, that you should do as I have done to you. Very truly,
I tell you, servants are not greater than their master, nor are messengers
greater than the one who sent them. If you know these things, you are
blessed if you do them" (Jn 13:12-17). Note how Jesus makes it clear that
even though he had just acted in the role of a slave, he still retains the
same status they thought he had: he is their teacher and Lord. He is not
flip-flopping roles here but helping them understand what it means to
be teacher and Lord. Contrary to their expectations, a true teacher and
Lord is someone who acts in humility and self-sacrificial love. For this
reason, if they are to live rightly with God, then they should imitate
these same traits and actions in their lives by performing the same
kinds of actions for others. They are Jesus' disciples, and they have been
sent by him out in to the world to partner with him in his mission. If

he uses his status in this way as he goes about his work, then they should do so as well.

Now we are in position to see the kind of practices and activities that go along with the discipline of theology. It is significant that John frames this episode around Jesus' internal reflections about his relationship with his Father and his saving mission as the eternal Son. Jesus' knowledge of these things—which he possesses by nature as God—is linked directly to his act of serving his disciples like a slave. At the very same moment that we see the "mind of Christ" reflecting on his own divine being and will, we see him performing acts of humility and self-sacrificial love. And if Christ always acts consistently with his own divine wisdom, then these actions show us what it looks like to possess this wisdom and live in correspondence to it. Here lies the lesson for those of us who practice theology. As people who have been united to Christ, we participate not only in his being but also in his mind. We know God by sharing in Christ's knowledge of God. And if Christ expressed his knowledge through these kinds of actions, then it makes sense that we should do the same thing. If we know God through Christ—and if we have been made participants in Christ as he continues to live out his eternal mission—then we should live like Christ by performing acts of humility and self-sacrificial love for others. This is what someone who rightly thinks and speaks about God looks like.

This means that a theologian seeking knowledge of God will do so faithfully when her pursuit of this knowledge is joined together with acts of self-giving love and humble service to others. John emphasizes the necessity of this kind of connection: "Whoever says, 'I have come to know him,' but does not obey his commandments is a liar, and in such a person the truth does not exist; but whoever obeys his word, truly in this person the love of God has reached perfection. By this we may be sure that we are in him: whoever says, 'I abide in him,' ought to walk just as he walked" (1 Jn 2:4-6). His point is that right and true knowledge of God always goes together with acts of obedience in the pattern of Christ. These actions cannot take place outside of our practice of theology, but within it. We cannot pursue theology and then act humbly on the side, serving people in the other areas of our life. No—being a faithful theologian includes following Christ in humility and obedience in and through the practice of theology itself. We pursue theological knowledge rightly when we do so for the sake of others, out of a desire to serve them by pointing them to God and sharing his love with them. As theologians, we should be known not for our arrogance or scholarly isolation but for the way we sacrificially love and serve the church and world through the practice of our discipline.

Acting in this way would be burdensome and overwhelming if it were an obligation that we had to meet under our own power. Yet this is not the case. We have been united to Christ, and he lives his own eternal life together with us. And the fact that he lowered himself to the floor to wash feet while reflecting on the reality that he was about to return to his Father in heaven tells us precisely how Jesus intends to live his eternal life: he is going to spend it giving himself to us in love so that we can live more faithfully with him. This is what he is doing even now at the Father's right hand, where "he always lives to make intercession" for us (Heb 7:25). From this position, Christ serves us by appealing on our behalf before the Father with the goal of equipping us to be faithful partners who work with him to fulfill God's plan. "Very truly, I tell you," Jesus says, "the one who believes in me will also do the works that I do and, in fact, will do greater works than these, because I am going to the Father. I will do whatever you ask in my name, so that the Father may be glorified in the Son. If in my name you ask me for anything, I will do it" (Jn 14:12-14).

Jesus intercedes for us in this way because we are no longer his servants but his "friends," people who exist in him, participate in his knowledge, partner with him in his mission and share his inheritance (Jn 15:15; Rom 8:17). And Christ does not intercede for us only in heaven but also on earth through his Spirit, who is sent to advocate on our behalf (Jn 15:26). As the very love of God himself "poured into our hearts" (Rom 5:5), the Spirit gives us the ability to think and act in the pattern of Christ's humility and obedience even though this runs against our fallen inclinations. "The Spirit helps us in our weakness" (Rom 8:26), and he does so precisely by prompting and enabling us to imitate the weakness of Christ before others so that we might show them the true nature of God's power. This leads us further along the pathway of discipleship and gives us confidence that we are headed toward the end for which God created us. "If we love one another," John says, "God lives in us, and his love is perfected in us. By this we know that we abide in him and he in us, because he has given us of his Spirit" (1 Jn 4:12-13).

A Spirit-filled life of humble, self-sacrificial love in the pattern of Jesus is the defining mark of a theologian who shares the mind of Christ. Our practice of theology does not merely complement our lives of discipleship to Jesus. This practice is itself a form of discipleship. As we learn more about God by reading Scripture and the works of other theologians in community with the Spirit, we are equipping ourselves to live, serve and partner with Christ in line with God's plan and the commission he has given us. We do not use our theological knowledge to build ourselves up, exercise power over others or take advantage of our status by utilizing the rights and privileges that come with such knowledge. We use it to build up other people, enrich the church and serve the world in Christ's name.

THINKING AFTER CHRIST

With this description of the defining characteristics of the theological life in hand, we can begin to think about how we might organize the method and practice of our discipline so that it corresponds to this kind of life. If being a disciple of Christ is following after Christ—and if the practice of theology takes place as we share the mind of Christ—then the discipline of theology should be the organized practice of thinking after Christ. We practice the discipline of theology in order to shape our thoughts so that they conform more and more closely to Christ's thoughts. We will know we are moving in the right direction when the pattern of thinking produced by our theology corresponds to the pattern of the incarnate Christ's thinking as he displayed it over the course of his life. And we can test whether or not our thinking is moving in this pattern by measuring whether or not our speech about God prompts acts of sacrificial love in the pattern of Christ's own acts of love.

This way of proceeding is especially useful for those who practice theology in academic settings, because it offers a natural point of contact between theology and the practice of other academic disciplines. For example, imagine that we were studying physics and wanted to learn Albert Einstein's theory of relativity. Obviously, if left to ourselves, very few of us could come up with this theory on our own. So, the discipline of physics is not organized in such a way that it leaves its students to figure out this theory for themselves. Instead, Einstein's ideas are presented, his proofs are used, and we are called to follow his intellectual lead. The assumption is that if we study Einstein's insights and trace out the reasoning he used to arrive at his theory, most of us will be able to come to some sort of basic understanding of it. This requires hard work, of course, along with careful instruction and intellectual growth. But the entire discipline of physics presumes that with properly organized teaching and a lot of effort, it is possible to think after Einstein and share his knowledge. The discipline of theology is organized in much the same way. Our task is to think Christ's thoughts after him so that we can begin to reason as he did. We do so because we know that Christ is "the wisdom of God" (1 Cor 1:24), and we believe that we can share in this wisdom when we think in the pattern of his own thoughts.

Yet Christ's identity as God and the unique content of divine wisdom mean that the way we think after Christ must differ from the way we think after Einstein. We can learn Einstein's theory of relativity by tracing out the logic of his thinking, working through his equations, studying about his life and thought and imitating him in every way possible. But we cannot participate in Einstein's mind, nor do we need to do so. To think after Einstein is to deal with a human thinker engaged in a discipline that reflects on created realities. Theology is different, because we are seeking knowledge of God. The act of imitating Jesus and studying the record of his thoughts is not enough, because the wisdom we seek from him transcends all creaturely being. His thoughts go beyond history and time, and they relate to every area of reality. And Christ is not just another human; he also is fully God. His wisdom also stands in contradiction to our own limited abilities, especially after the effects of sin have left our minds "darkened" (Rom 1:21). Even though the task of thinking after Christ includes many of the same activities involved in our thinking after Einstein, we have to operate on a different register, because we have to be raised beyond our finite and fallen capacities in order to think as Christ does.

Fortunately, we were made in, through and for Christ (Col 1:16), and he has taken our human nature on himself and incorporated our lives into his own. We have our "life in Christ," as Paul says, "who became for us wisdom from God, and righteousness and sanctification and redemption" (1 Cor 1:30). Christ overcomes our sin and enables us think after him by allowing us to participate in his own life and thoughts. Of course, this participation does not come naturally to us because we do not instinctively think like Christ. We sometimes resist the knowledge Christ gives us through our participation in him, and this means we sometimes misunderstand what God has revealed to us in Christ or intentionally ignore it to go our own way.

The reality of these sinful tendencies helps us to see more clearly how the discipline of theology should be organized. Because we are "estranged and hostile in mind" toward God and unfit for the task we are trying to perform (Col 1:21), we must proceed under the assumption that we are not free to determine how our discipline operates. Our knowledge of God does not result from an act of our will, as if we can know God simply because we want to do so. Nor is learning theology something that happens automatically as the inevitable result of acquiring a certain level of knowledge or expertise. Rather, our study of theology will be organized rightly only when it proceeds from the reality that all true knowledge of God comes to us as a gift of grace. As Thomas Aquinas puts it, our knowledge of God is not the result of an "inquiry of natural reason that demonstrates what is believed," but rather, it is the product of an "inquiry into those things whereby a man is induced to believe."[9] God makes us capable of knowing him. He does so by giving us a "supernatural participation in the divine goodness" through Christ and the

[9]Aquinas, *Summa Theologica* II-II, q. 2, a. 1, ad. 1.

Spirit, a double grace that gives us the ability to know God even though we are incapable of, and unfit for, this knowledge.[10] The discipline of theology is ordered around God's grace when it proceeds from the presupposition that we know God only as God reveals himself to us in the saving history of Christ and the Spirit. And because we come to know Christ through the hearing of the gospel and our Spirit-propelled response of faith, we can begin there—with our faith in Christ by the power of the Spirit.

The fact that we know God only by grace through faith reminds us that we been given true knowledge of an incomprehensible God. This gives us a sense of what we can and cannot do as theologians. Because Christ leads us to knowledge of the God "whom no one has ever seen or can see" (1 Tim 6:16)—and because Christ himself comes to us as a "mystery" (Col 4:3)—we have to practice our discipline knowing from the outset that we will never obtain the knowledge we seek within our lifetime. Our conception of what is possible for our theological work is limited by the reality that God will always remain beyond our ability to grasp fully. This limitation does not mean that we should not seek to know God, but instead it shows us that our task is to be obedient by seeking to know everything we can know on the basis of what has been revealed. In fact, in a certain sense the act of seeking is itself the goal of our work, because this act produces the exact kind of intellectual and moral formation God desires us to have. Put differently: the practice of theology should be ordered around the goal of seeking God rather than finding him precisely because the act of seeking is what forms us to adopt the humble way of life that corresponds to the mind of Christ.

This way of practicing theology overlaps with our life of discipleship more generally. A theologian who is seeking knowledge of God by grace through faith is going to be a person who walks the way of Jesus, because anyone who seeks to know God is going to be pursuing the mind of Christ and the activities of humility and obedience that go along with it. The discipline of theology should be organized in such a way that its

---

[10]Aquinas, *Summa Theologica* II-II, q. 2., a. 3.

practice promotes this kind of mindset and rewards this way of life. Paul provides a helpful template in this regard when he says that his entire life is ordered around the "surpassing value of knowing Christ Jesus" (Phil 3:8). He knows that he has not yet obtained this knowledge fully, nor will he do so in this life; even so, however, he continues to seek after it: "I press on to make it my own, because Christ Jesus has made me his own" (Phil 3:12). This verse aptly describes the posture of theologians: we seek to know God because we have been claimed by God in the fulfillment of God's eternal plan to unite his life to ours through Christ and the Spirit. Even though this knowledge will be given to us only in the future, the fact that our participation in this future is secured by Christ and sealed by the Spirit means that we can seek it freely now by thinking after Christ. We do not have the burden of figuring out everything there is to know or answering every question. Our job is to think about God as best we can and then share what we have learned with others.

To pursue theology in this way is to believe that our practice of theology is a form of communion with God as much as it is about acquiring new insights and information. After all, we are not seeking knowledge of an *it* but a *you*, a distinct personal subject who addresses us and whom we address in return. This exchange of words—a personal exchange occurring between two agents, one divine and one human—means that theology fits directly in line with God's plan for our existence. Practicing theology is one of the ways we anticipate the life of fellowship we will share with God for eternity. Despite the hard work and mystery involved, our theological work uplifts us, because to think and speak about God in the way of Christ is to believe that we are headed toward the day when our minds will be redeemed and renewed in him.

Paul reflects this kind of mindset when he says that we are to "seek the things that are above, where Christ is, seated at the right hand of God." We should do so, he explains, because we exist in Christ: "for you have died, and your life with hidden with Christ in God. When Christ who is your life is revealed, then you also will be revealed with him in glory" (Col 3:1-4). One of the interesting parts of this claim is the notion that our hidden lives will be fully revealed when Christ himself is revealed.

Paul is hinting that, because of Christ, we are defined by realities and truths that exceed what we can see and know in the present. The fact that we live in and through Christ, and he lives in and through us, means that there is more to us than meets the eye. We are participants in the very life of God through Christ and the Spirit even now, although we can scarcely see it and hardly believe it. This insight helps us to grasp the implications of Paul's claim that "our citizenship is in heaven, and it is from there that we are expecting a Savior, the Lord Jesus Christ. He will transform the body of our humiliation that it may be conformed to the body of his glory, by the power that also enables him to make all things subject to himself" (Phil 3:20-21). The practice of theology is one of the ways we begin to live in correspondence to this hope. As we know more about God through Christ, and as the Spirit gifts us with new knowledge and understanding of God and his eternal plan, we begin to realize more and more who we truly are. Theology is an exercise in discovering the reality behind all things, including the reality that we are people who were chosen in Christ before the foundation of the world.

This means that, at its core, theology is a discipline ordered by hope. We engage in theology in the belief that, one day, we will know God and receive the inheritance that comes with being his children; that we will transcend the limits of our finite nature and share in his own divine knowledge; and that we will do so in a world that will be fully ordered around God's wisdom. In the meantime, as the recipients of God's grace who have been called to follow Jesus, our task is to "run with perseverance the race that is set before us, looking to Jesus the pioneer and perfecter of our faith." He is the one in whom we believe, because he is the one who lived a perfect life, "endured the cross" and now lives as the resurrected Son sitting "at the right hand of the throne of God" (Heb 12:1-2). As theologians, we follow Christ by thinking after Christ. He does not give us every answer, much like he did not tell the disciples where they were going. He just said, "Follow me." And we do, thinking all along the way.

seven

THEOLOGY IN CHRIST

☙

To describe the context in which theology can be practiced faithfully is one thing, but to practice it faithfully is another. This brings us back to the concerns that many Christians have about the discipline of theology and its relationship to the church. They worry that theology distracts us from the most important activities of the Christian life by inhibiting rather than enabling our discipleship to Jesus Christ. The discipline either undermines our faith by raising questions we cannot answer or leads us away from obedience by making us overconfident and contentious. The result is a divided church full of theological partisans who have ceased to focus on Jesus and instead serve their own interests.

With a rebuilt framework for the practice of theology now in hand, our challenge is to offer a picture of what it looks like to live as theologians who serve the church as faithful disciples of Jesus Christ. In this picture, we are theologians who live on our knees before God, with an open Bible in front of us and the voice of the church in our ears. We pray for the Spirit to illumine our minds to help us understand what God has revealed and imitate Christ's humble obedience so that we can think and speak rightly in partnership with him for the sake of the church and its mission. We listen to the voices of those outside the church by hearing their questions, accepting their critiques and learning from them with humility and graciousness. We participate in the world by making its joys, sorrows and hopes our own as we love it in the same way that we love ourselves. And we keep our eyes fixed on Jesus, the risen Lord, the one in whom we live and the one who lives in and through us.

The goal of this chapter is give more resolution to this picture by presenting nine characteristics that distinguish the life of someone who practices theology faithfully within the context of God's saving work in Christ and the Spirit. The characteristics offered here are not exhaustive, but they are representative. A theologian who knows God through participation in the mind of Christ and who lives obediently by the power of the Spirit will demonstrate these kinds of qualities and engage in these sorts of actions.

1. We practice theology as disciples when we measure our thinking and speaking about God by the person and work of Jesus Christ as revealed in Scripture.

When Jesus says, "I am the way, and the truth, and the life" (Jn 14:6), he makes it clear that right knowledge of God comes to us personally in and through his presence. Even though he stands "far above all rule and authority and power and dominion, and above every name that is named"—and even though God has put "all things under his feet and has made him the head over all things" (Eph 1:21-22)—Jesus still comes to us directly and intimately. He meets us, as Dietrich Bonhoeffer says, "not as timeless truth, but rather as truth breaking into a concrete moment, as God's speaking to us . . . God's Word personally addressed to the human being, calling him to responsibility."[1]

This idea seems odd for us, as Philip shows when he responds by asking Jesus, on behalf of the disciples, to "show us the Father" (Jn 14:8). The disciples do not understand: they know Jesus, but now they want to know God. Jesus directs Philip back to himself. "Have I been with you all this time, Philip, and you still do not know me? Whoever has seen me has seen the Father. How can you say, 'Show us the Father'?" (Jn 14:9). Jesus wants them to recognize that they have true knowledge of God because they know him. There is no other way to God because he alone can show them the Father. "All things have been handed over to me by my Father," Jesus says, "and no one knows the Son except the Father, and

---

[1]Dietrich Bonhoeffer, "Lectures in Christology," in *Berlin: 1932–1933*, Dietrich Bonhoeffer Works, vol. 12, ed. Larry L. Rasmussen (Minneapolis: Fortress, 2009), 317.

no one knows the Father except the Son and anyone to whom the Son chooses to reveal him" (Mt 11:27). Only a personal encounter with Jesus can give us the knowledge that leads to eternal life with God.

Jesus encounters us today chiefly in and through the words of Scripture. Paul reflects this reality when he reminds Timothy about "the sacred writings that are able to instruct you for salvation through faith in Christ Jesus" (2 Tim 3:15). The connection Paul draws between Scripture and Christ is instructive. Even though the Bible was written in a very different time and place than ours, God speaks to us through it to bring us to salvation in Christ. If we hold ourselves back from Scripture—treating it as if it were merely an object to be studied or a resource from which to draw truths that then can be applied to our lives—then we are shutting ourselves off from this divine speech and its purpose. God speaks to us personally through Scripture, not only to inform us about the true nature of reality but also to call us to live in this reality and make it our home.[2]

This fits the pattern of God's work throughout salvation history. God came to Abraham and called him to a new land (Gen 12:1-2); he reached out to Moses and commanded him to lead Israel out of Egypt (Ex 3:4-10); and he informed Samuel that judgment was coming (1 Sam 3:4-14). Jesus repeats this pattern when he finds his disciples and calls them to follow him even though they do not know where he is going. And Jesus issues this same call every time the Word of God is proclaimed to us. "For the first disciples of Jesus," Bonhoeffer says, "it was also not as if they first recognized him as the Christ, and then received his command. Rather, it was only through his word and his command that they recognized him."[3] And like every call of God—from Abraham to Moses to Samuel—the command that comes to us from Christ is the same: "it demands faith from an undivided heart, and love of God and neighbor with all our heart and soul."[4] This is the call with which theology begins and proceeds. To participate in the mind of Christ is to have our own minds shaped and

---

[2]On this point, see Karl Barth, "The New World in the Bible," in *The Word of God and Theology*, trans. Amy Marga (London: T&T Clark, 2011), 15-29.

[3]Dietrich Bonhoeffer, *Discipleship*, Dietrich Bonhoeffer Works, vol. 4, ed. John D. Godsey and Geffrey B. Kelly (Minneapolis: Fortress, 2001), 202.

[4]Ibid., 203.

directed by Christ's call to faith and obedience. Because Christ uses Scripture as his instrument to issue this call, we have to approach the text itself as a living Word. We have to read it in the expectation that—because Christ himself speaks to us in it—this Word will overwhelm us, reform us and move us to some place new.

Christ comes to us as the criterion, not only to the true knowledge of God but also to true knowledge of ourselves and all things. "We can no longer speak about our life other than in this relation to Jesus Christ," Bonhoeffer says. "Apart from Christ as the origin, essence, and goal of life, of our life, and apart from the fact that we are creatures who are reconciled and redeemed, we can only arrive at biological or ideological abstractions."[5] No gift we receive from God—whether it be the gift of our being or the gift of our own thinking—happens apart from Christ. He defines everything because his life is the measure of all being and truth. "We know that the Son of God has come and has given us understanding so that we may know him who is true," John says, "and we are in him who is true, in his Son Jesus Christ. He is the true God and eternal life" (1 Jn 5:20). God's eternal plan is that we come to know the truth by sharing in the life of Jesus. "For those whom he foreknew he also predestined to be conformed to the image of his Son," Paul says, "in order that he might be the firstborn within a large family" (Rom 8:29). We are made children of God as we are made like Jesus and given a share in his knowledge and the actions that flow from it. Our calling as theologians is to bear witness to this life in Jesus through our love for God and others. And we do so through Jesus himself, because he does not hold himself back from us but gives himself to us again and again, forming us through his Word and Spirit, so that we might live before God and share in his love.

2. We practice theology as disciples when our thinking stays within the limits of our faith in Jesus Christ.

If we want to keep our theology centered on Jesus Christ, then the place to begin is where our participation in Christ begins: with the faith

---

[5]Dietrich Bonhoeffer, *Ethics*, Dietrich Bonhoeffer Works, vol. 6, ed. Clifford Green (Minneapolis: Fortress, 2005), 251.

that comes from hearing the gospel (Rom 10:17). John Calvin defines faith as the knowledge of "God's benevolence toward us, founded upon the truth of the freely given promise in Christ, both revealed to our minds and sealed upon our hearts through the Holy Spirit."[6] As we have seen, because this knowledge of God comes through Christ and the Spirit, it is intrinsically related to a life of discipleship to Christ lived by the power of his Spirit. And because faith involves our response to the good news about Jesus, the knowledge we have through faith is personal in nature. To have faith is not merely to believe certain things about Christ but to trust in Christ himself as the Spirit enables.

We stay within the limits of faith by recognizing that even though we know the truth about God through Christ, we know this truth as a mystery that transcends our understanding. We would have to become Christ, rather than participate in him, in order to know God in the same way he does. And unlike some other academic disciplines where the scholar both sets the agenda and determines the method, we are not in control of the knowledge we gain or how we proceed. Christ himself governs these things by leading us to Scripture and guiding us by his Spirit. He gives us knowledge "to the extent that our salvation requires and our capacity allows," and we stay within the limits of our faith when we go no further than where he takes us.[7] Our lack of control gives us both a posture of humility and a hesitancy to speculate beyond what Christ has shown us through his life and speech. "Everyone who does not abide in the teaching of Christ," John says, "but goes beyond it, does not have God" (2 Jn 9). To stay within these limits is to embrace the reality of God's mystery and to proceed knowing that many of our claims cannot be confirmed in this life. "While we teach that faith ought to be certain and assured," Calvin explains, "we cannot imagine any certainty that is not tinged with doubt, or any assurance that is not assailed by some anxiety."[8]

---

[6]Calvin, *Institutes of the Christian Religion*, 3.2.7.

[7]John Calvin, *Commentary on 2 Corinthians* 3:18, in *The Second Epistle of Paul the Apostle to the Corinthians and the Epistles to Timothy, Titus and Philemon*, trans. T. A. Smail (Grand Rapids: Eerdmans, 1964), 50.

[8]Calvin, *Institutes of the Christian Religion*, 3.2.17.

For all of these reasons, we make a mistake if we think our task as theologians is to create a system that removes all mystery, erases all doubt and answers every doctrinal question. Such an approach betrays a misunderstanding of Peter's instruction to "always be ready to make your defense to anyone who demands from you an accounting for the hope that is in you" (1 Pet 3:15). Certainly, we must be able to explain the reasons for our faith and why it is not irrational to hold it. Yet the ability to give these sorts of defenses does not mean that we have to answer every objection that comes to us. Peter reflects this insight in the next verse when he says that we should give our defense with "gentleness and reverence" (1 Pet 3:16). To proceed with reverence means to think and speak with an awareness of our place in relation to God. He is the Creator, and we are his creatures. God knows himself perfectly by nature; we have our knowledge only by the grace which elevates our finite and fallen minds. And while God has perfect knowledge from eternity, our knowledge comes to us gradually as God fulfills his plan in "the fullness of time" (Eph 1:10). This means, as Calvin puts it, that we cannot seek "comprehension of the sort that is commonly concerned with those things which fall under human perception."[9] To practice theology in this way would be to turn from the reality of God's grace and to turn toward an idol of our speculative reason, crafted in our own image.

We rest our claims on God's grace by basing them on Scripture, knowing that its authors wrote these texts so that we might both "know the truth" (Lk 1:4) and "have eternal life" (1 Jn 5:13). While many of our statements come straight from Scripture, many others also go beyond it as we make connections that work out the implications of Scripture's claims. We proceed knowing that our primary task is not to develop a comprehensive theological system but to think systematically about what God has revealed, discerning what must be true about God, creation and our own lives in light of everything God has said and done. We make our theological claims knowing that, at best, they are provisional place-holders for the ones we will make on the day when we see Christ face to

---

[9]Ibid., 3.2.14.

face (1 Jn 3:2). As such, our claims take "the character of an offering" as we place them before God in humility and pray that he finds them acceptable and pleasing in his sight.[10]

All of this means that we ought to become increasingly humble—rather than arrogant—the more we practice theology. Humility comes because we know that the more we say the closer we move to the limits of what we ought to say, and that one day, we will stand before God to hear him confirm or deny that what we have said is true. The prospect of this judgment means that the practice of theology properly takes the form of an act of obedience offered in faith and hope. As such, it stands in a long line of similar acts. Hebrews offers several examples of people who obeyed God even though their knowledge of God rested on faith rather than sight. Noah showed faith when he obeyed God's commands to build an ark even though he was doing so in preparation for "events as yet unseen" (Heb 11:7). So did Abraham when he set out for a new land while "not knowing where he was going" (Heb 11:8), and again when he believed God's promise that he would have many descendants "even though he was too old" and his wife was barren (Heb 11:11). The list goes on, from Moses to David to Samuel and others. In each case, these persons "died in faith without having received the promises, but from a distance they saw and greeted them" (Heb 11:13).

These figures are counted faithful because they believed and obeyed God's command even though they did not fully comprehend it. To be a theologian is to walk down the same path. Even though we do not see God directly, we seek to be obedient by offering claims about God on the basis of what God has said and done in Christ and the Spirit in the trust that God will count us faithful in the attempt.

3. We practice theology as disciples when we seek to live obediently in the pattern of the incarnate Jesus Christ's obedience to God.

Because our knowledge of God comes through our participation in the mind of Christ, it makes sense that the practice of theology will be

---

[10]Karl Barth, *Evangelical Theology: An Introduction*, trans. Grover Foley (New York: Holt, Rinehart and Winston, 1963), 166.

linked directly to acts of obedience that stand in line with Christ's actions. Jesus himself said this should be the case. From his point of view, faith and obedience always go together: "the one who believes in me will also do the works that I do" (Jn 14:12). Paul calls this the "obedience of faith" (Rom 1:5), and he argues that it reflects God's plan for us, because we were "created in Christ Jesus for good works, which God prepared beforehand to be our way of life" (Eph 2:10). Such statements indicate that a theologian who thinks and speaks rightly about God will be one who also lives a holy life before God in the pattern of Christ.

On one level, the connection between our thoughts and deeds is practical. When seeking to know an object, it helps to get as close as you can to that object. Theologians are seeking to know God, and so he is the object of our knowledge. And yet he comes to us not as an object but as a living and active subject who meets us in the midst of his divine plan to save us through the Son and the Spirit. As we are caught up with them and begin to reflect their work, we begin to correspond more closely to God and are in position to know him better. If we turn away from their work and live in contradiction to it, we are likely not to recognize God or know him when he comes to us. Athanasius draws the analogy of a person who wishes "to see the light of the sun." He "would certainly wipe and clear his eyes, purifying himself to be almost like that which he desires."[11] Theologians seeking to know God would make similar preparations by seeking to "purify themselves, just as he is pure" in order to receive this knowledge rightly (1 Jn 3:3).

This purification takes the form of a life of obedience to God lived in the pattern of Jesus. But we do not pursue this life alone. Jesus promised that he would be with us, propelling us along the way through the power of the Spirit's indwelling presence. He fulfills this promise from the moment that we first hear the gospel, for it comes to us "not in word only, but also in power and in the Holy Spirit" (1 Thess 1:5). The Spirit serves as the point of connection between our faith and obedience, as Paul indicates when he links "belief in the truth" to our "sanctification by the

---

[11]Athanasius, *On the Incarnation*, paragraph 57, trans. John Behr (Crestwood, NY: St. Vladimir's Seminary Press, 2011), 110.

Spirit" (2 Thess 2:13). And the Spirit does not work simply to make us holy and leave it at that; rather, he equips us to work as Christ's partners. Our obedience to Christ matters because God's plan is for us to "work together with" Christ to fulfill the mission God has given us as Christ's body (2 Cor 6:1).

A lack of obedience signifies that even though we may know a lot of information, we do not really know God. Theologians are especially susceptible to committing the error of thinking that knowledge of God can be divorced from a corresponding life of obedience. James laments those who hear the Word and then "deceive themselves" that merely possessing this knowledge is enough. We also must be "doers of the word," he insists (Jas 1:22). This reflects the reality that when we fail to live in the pattern of Jesus, we contradict our participation in Christ's mind. "If we say that we have fellowship with him while we are walking in darkness," John says, "we lie and do not do what is true" (1 Jn 1:6). In fact, Paul labels those who "profess to know God" but "deny him by their actions" as "detestable, disobedient, unfit for any good work" (Tit 1:16). He thinks that, since being in Christ involves being a new creation, our actions have to reflect this newness. "Truth is in Jesus," he says, and so, like Jesus, we must clothe ourselves in "true righteousness and holiness" (Eph 4:21, 24).

The implications of having knowledge without obedience are reflected in a striking story in Luke 10.[12] One day while Jesus is teaching, a scholar tests him with a question: "What must I do to inherit eternal life?" (Lk 10:25). Luke hints that this question is hostile, because he uses the same word, "test," to describe the devil's testing of Jesus in the wilderness (Lk 4:12). Likely sensing the scholar's antagonism, Jesus does not respond directly but instead asks the scholar two questions of his own. "What is written in the law? What do you read there?" (Lk 10:26). Jesus' questions are carefully framed. He is asking the scholar not only what he knows but also how—or in what way—he knows it.

The scholar gets the *what* part of the answer exactly right: "You shall

---

[12]The reading of this passage offered here is drawn from the interpretation found in Eugene Peterson, *Eat This Book: A Conversation in the Art of Spiritual Reading* (Grand Rapids: Eerdmans, 2006), 83-84.

love the Lord your God with all your heart, and with all your soul, and with all your strength, and with all your mind; and your neighbor as yourself." Jesus affirms his answer: "You have given the right answer; do this, and you will live." But Luke makes it clear that Jesus' command that the scholar should act upon what he knows strikes the scholar in the wrong way. "But wanting to justify himself, he asked Jesus, 'And who is my neighbor?' " (Lk 10:27-29). We can only speculate, but the fact that the scholar asks the question to "justify himself" likely indicates that he was not fully obeying this commandment. He knew the truth about what God wanted him to do, but he did not live in line with his knowledge. His question likely betrays an unwillingness to alter his behavior. He seeks a precise definition of "neighbor" so he can understand who and what a neighbor is on his own terms. This is the classic move of a scholar, one that theologians often make. The scholar knows that if he can determine the exact parameters of the definition, he probably can find a way to justify his lack of obedience to the command by saying that only certain people fit the definition of a neighbor.[13]

The problem with this kind of qualification is that it leaves the scholar in control of how to obey God's command. He will have used his theological knowledge to fit God into his view of the world rather than conforming his life to what God has revealed. Jesus sees this problem immediately, and so instead of debating the meaning of the concept "neighbor," he tells the parable of the Good Samaritan (Lk 10:30-35). In light of the story of how the Samaritan cares for the wounded man after a priest and a Levite pass him by, Jesus asks the scholar: "Which of these three, do you think, was a neighbor to the man who fell into the hands of the robbers?" The scholar said, "The one who showed him mercy." Jesus said to him, "Go and do likewise" (Lk 10:36-37). Note how Jesus' parable prevents the scholar from turning his neighbor into a depersonalized intellectual concept which could be debated—and thus manipulated—and instead leads him to face the implications of his knowledge of God. Jesus places a stark choice before the scholar: now that he knows

---

[13]See Peterson, *Eat This Book*, 84.

the truth about God and his commandment, his only choice is to obey or disobey. There are no qualifications, and there is no way to know or live rightly with God apart from this obedience.[14]

The point of this episode, and its relevance for those of us practicing theology, is that having the right information about God is not enough. To know God is to live with God, and to live rightly with God, we must make the choice to reflect God's qualities and character in our words and deeds. God gives us knowledge not so that we can simply know it but so that we will use it to follow him in obedience. "For obedience," Karl Barth says, "is the purpose and goal of hearing."[15] There is no way to practice theology rightly apart from such obedience, because there is no way to participate in the mind of Christ without participating in the rest of him, including his life of obedient deeds. We cannot divorce our knowledge from this obedience, or qualify it in some way, as if our actions take place in some separate realm of practical application that has no relation to our thinking. The highest levels of theology and the most practical acts of obedience go together.

They align so closely, in fact, that when organized and practiced properly, theology should propel us into obedience. Peter reflects this when he tells believers to prepare their "minds for action" (1 Pet 1:13), as does Hebrews when it describes a mature Christian as someone "whose faculties have been trained by practice to distinguish good from evil" (Heb 5:14). Studying theology is one way we can engage in this kind of preparation and training. As we learn to think and speak rightly about God, we become prepared to act in obedience to God and trained to make correct judgments about him. In this manner, our theological work itself becomes a form of obedience. To practice theology rightly is to live more fully into Paul's command to be "transformed by the renewing of your minds, so that you may discern what is the will of God—what is good and acceptable and perfect" (Rom 12:2).

To think in this way is not to water down theology or make it less intellectually rigorous. Even in its most academic forms, theology is practiced

---

[14]Ibid.
[15]Karl Barth, *Church Dogmatics* II/2 (Edinburgh: T&T Clark, 1957), 30.

rightly only when our minds are remade by Christ and our wills are redirected by the Spirit. By its very nature, theology is a spiritual discipline,
and God uses it to bring our entire lives, not just our minds, into conformity with his being and plan. "Good theologians," John Webster says,
"are those whose life and thought are caught up in the process of being
slain and made alive by the gospel, and of acquiring and exercising habits
of mind and heart which take very seriously the gospel's provocation."[16]
The formation of these habits is gradual but transformational. As we
participate in the mind of Christ and know God through him, we develop the habit of seeing other people and the world around us as Christ
himself does. And as we learn to surrender control of our intellectual
agenda, we become accustomed to having the kind of humility that
makes us more willing to serve God and others rather than ourselves.
This means that theology need not be in tension with discipleship to
Jesus; it is one of the ways we can become a better disciple because it is,
in fact, a form of discipleship.

4. We practice theology as disciples when we do our theological work for the benefit of others.

Our desire to learn and teach theology can be rooted in either false or
true motives. Negatively, Paul talks about those who "proclaim Christ
from envy and rivalry" as well as "selfish ambition" (Phil 1:15-17). He
warns Timothy that some people are "conceited" and have "a morbid
craving for controversy and disputes about words." As a result, they are
"depraved in mind and bereft of the truth" (1 Tim 6:4-5). He also says that
some seek to gain knowledge of God to further themselves. Like Adam
and Eve, they want knowledge on their own terms, so they can satisfy
their "itching ears" and justify their desire to "turn away from listening
to the truth" (2 Tim 4:3-4). James echoes this assessment and criticizes
those who seek knowledge of God, and prompt debates about it, for their
own selfish gain: "You want something and do not have it . . . so you
engage in disputes and conflicts" (Jas 4:2). Others pursue learning to gain
stature and win favor. Gregory Nazianzus compares such people with

---

[16]John Webster, "Habits: Cultivating the Theologian's Soul," Stimulus 7, no. 1 (February 1999): 16.

cheap entertainers. In their "obsession with setting and solving conun-
drums," he says, they act like "the promoters of wrestling-bouts in the
theaters . . . the sort of which are stage-managed to give the uncritical
spectators visual sensations and compel their applause." In this sense,
their theological knowledge is more of a "social accomplishment" than
an act of discipleship.[17]

In contrast, those who learn and teach with true motives do so "from
goodwill" and "out of love" (Phil 1:15-17). Paul regularly points to himself
as an example in this regard, explaining that his teaching does not "spring
from deceit or impure motives" but out of a desire "to please God who
tests our hearts" (1 Thess 2:3-4). He instructs others not for his own
benefit but in the pattern of Christ's own sacrificial love. He tells the
Thessalonians, for instance, that he never sought to flatter them or win
praise from them. And even though he could have "made demands"
based on his status as an apostle, he did not do so. Rather, he chose to
approach them gently, "like a nurse tenderly caring for her own children,"
sharing not only his teaching but also his very self with them out of love
(1 Thess 2:5-8). This kind of approach reflects Christ-like humility, because the goal of our teaching is not to build up ourselves as theologians
but to serve and enrich others.[18] Such motivations, as we have seen, reflect God's own being and character. This is why those who teach with
such motives do so "as persons sent from God and standing in his
presence" (2 Cor 2:17).

As theologians, we will know that we have adopted this kind of posture
when our practice of theology produces the Spirit's fruits of humility,
love, patience and generosity in our lives and in those of the people with
whom we interact. We reflect the fruit of humility when we do our best
to "avoid stupid controversies" that stem from a desire to be right, win
an argument or prove our superiority (Tit 3:9). It is particularly displayed
in the way we treat others. Theologians who live in humility approach

[17]Gregory Nazianzus, Oration 27.2-3, from *On God and Christ: The Five Theological Orations and Two Letters to Cledonius*, trans. Fredrick Williams and Lionel Wickham (Crestwood, NY: St. Vladimir's Seminary Press, 2002), 25-27.
[18]See Michael Gorman, *Cruciformity: Paul's Narrative Spirituality of the Cross* (Grand Rapids: Eerdmans, 2001), 192-95.

the task of instruction not with an air of superiority but out of a desire
to share the truth (2 Tim 2:15). We instruct others in order to serve them
rather than stand over them or put them in their place. Even if we engage
in a heated theological debate with fellow believers—as we sometimes
must—we reflect pure motives when we speak to them graciously and
seek to help rather than harm them (Col 4:6). We "avoid wrangling over
words" with others (2 Tim 2:14), even if this means withdrawing from a
debate or refusing to win every point. Our humility also is displayed
whenever we refuse to speculate or pretend that we know more than we
do out of a desire to prove ourselves, win favor or defeat an opponent.

We reflect the fruit of love when we relate to others in the pattern of
Christ's own love. His love for us is not defined primarily in terms of his
feeling or desire but by his willingness to give himself for our benefit.
"God's love was revealed among us in this way," John says. "God sent his
only Son into the world so that we might live through him. In this is love,
not that we loved God but that he loved us and sent his Son to be the
atoning sacrifice for our sins" (1 Jn 4:9-10). As those who exist in Christ,
we reflect his love when we freely give ourselves to others in love for their
benefit. "Beloved, since God loved us so much, we also ought to love one
another" (1 Jn 4:11). The opposite of Christlike love is not hate but self-
ishness. We fail to love like Christ whenever we hold ourselves back from
others or when we become self-referential in our thinking. This posture
often goes together with a certain kind of conceit, as well as a tendency
to view others as our competition (Gal 5:26). Rather than dedicating
ourselves to enriching the lives of others, our thoughts and actions tend
to revolve around our own needs and a desire to establish a position of
power over others. Often a failure to love occurs in concert with a life of
idolatry, which is marked by a tendency to turn inward and indulge ourselves in the name of God.

The primary place where theologians pursue Christ-like love is within
the church, because the church's existence is defined by the love its
members share for one another and for the world. We especially display
love for others when we offer theological instruction in order to enrich
and benefit the church so its members might relate to God more faith-

fully. To proceed in this way is to see the recipients of our instruction as inherently valuable, God's own people chosen and called to carry out his eternal plan. As we relate to them, our goal is that our teaching reflects Paul's description of love: "it does not insist on its own way; it is not irritable or resentful; it does not rejoice in wrongdoing, but rejoices in the truth. It bears all things, believes all things, hopes all things, endures all things" (1 Cor 13:5-7). We practice theology faithfully when we share our insights to build other people up, to encourage them and to sustain them in their faith in the hope that God might use our efforts and their lives for his purposes.

We demonstrate patience when we persist in seeking the knowledge of God even when it is difficult and discouraging. We do so because we know that our pursuit of theology is not about our own happiness or security but about God's call that we use our work to enrich and equip others. This call keeps our minds focused. When Paul tells us to concentrate our thoughts on that which is noble, right, pure, lovely and admirable (Phil 4:8-9), he is giving us the key to patience: we refuse to allow ourselves to be discouraged or disheartened but work for others in the hope that God will use what we do for their benefit. This mindset also can help us learn to be patient with ourselves, particularly when we are confused or make mistakes. Theological errors often stem from impatience, which manifests itself in an unwillingness to adhere to what God has revealed. We reflect God's patience when we refuse to speculate. We also do so when we refuse to accept an easy or trite answer but put in the time and work to think more deeply about an issue by continuing to study Scripture and listen to the voice of the church.

Theologians display patience by giving others the space to learn and grow, especially when we know that they disagree with us. We should embrace those who reject our views and refuse to be easily offended. The criticism of others cannot define our relationship with them, but rather, we must see such moments as a chance to display unconditional love. And as God has been patient with us—by sustaining us even after our sin and by acting to save us—so we must be patient with doctrinal error when we encounter it. We reflect the Spirit when we are not "quickly shaken in mind or alarmed" by someone's theological mistake (2 Thess 2:2). We do not see their errors as an opportunity to criticize others or stand over against them in self-righteousness. Rather, we display patience when we engage them out of a sincere love for their well-being. We reflect Christ when we commit to walk beside them in their naiveté and wrongheadedness, refusing to bid them farewell but embracing them in humility and love.

The fruit of generosity manifests itself in our lives when we measure the value of our theological work primarily by how it can contribute to the flourishing of others. "We are speaking in Christ before God," Paul says. "Everything we do, beloved, is for the sake of building you up" (2 Cor 12:19). Even though our pursuit of theological knowledge often takes much effort and comes with a personal cost, we refuse to focus on what we can gain but on what we can give. This begins by giving our intellect over to God so he can reshape and reform it for his service. It continues as we engage the work of others generously by listening to what they have to say, treating their ideas with respect and giving honest feedback while also offering them the benefit of the doubt. We begin by presuming that every theologian we interact with is just as faithful as we are, and loves Christ just as much as we do, until we can prove otherwise. This is part of what it means to "regard no one from a human point of view" but to see them in light of Christ (2 Cor 5:16). And because we assume that they, too, are joined to Christ and filled with his Spirit, we try to outdo one another in showing honor to them (Rom 12:10). This kind of generosity is especially needed when we engage with figures from the past, who may think quite differently than us. As C. S. Lewis notes, every age has a "characteristic blindness" on some matter that produces "untroubled agreement" among everyone at the time.[19] Our age is no exception. We show generosity by allowing other voices, especially those coming from places different than our own, to critique us. We open ourselves to others by giving them our work and receiving feedback from them. Among other things, this displays that we have a heart "wide open," with no re-

---

[19]C. S. Lewis, "Preface," in Athanasius, *On the Incarnation* (Crestwood, NY: St. Vladimir's Seminary Press, 2011), 11.

striction in our affection for them and a willingness to be changed by our encounter with them (2 Cor 6:11).

5. We practice theology as disciples when we use our theological work to serve the church and its mission.

Theologians serve the church primarily by offering instruction with the goal of helping the church's members to follow Christ in faith and obedience. Such instruction is critically important for the health of the church's members. Many people disengage from the church or fail to pursue its mission not because they reject Christ but because they find the church's teachings and mission irrelevant. "The chief challenge facing the church now," Robert Jenson says, "is not unbelief, but incomprehension. Those who reject it do not do so because they find it false but because they find it uninteresting, pointless, obscure, unimportant."[20] This perception often stems from their lack of understanding of the faith, which itself flows from the false assumption that it can be immediately comprehended by anyone. Yet from the beginning, the apostles taught that even though the gospel can be grasped by anyone through the power of the Spirit, a deep understanding of the faith requires careful instruction and sustained effort. Paul tells the Corinthians that he approached them as "infants in Christ," feeding them with spiritual milk because they were "not ready for solid food" (1 Cor 3:1-2). Theologians exist in order to contribute to the process of helping the members move from milk to food.

This process can be challenging, in part, because some church members are hesitant to receive theological training. As Augustine explains, they "get angry and think they are being insulted, and very often they prefer to believe that the ones they hear it from have nothing really to say, rather than consider themselves unable to grasp what they say."[21] As theologians, we respond properly by not dismissing these reactions as foolish or naive but by seeing them as reminders that we must approach our work with humility and a willingness to serve. Because we

---

[20]Robert Jenson, *The Knowledge of Things Hoped For* (New York: Oxford University Press, 1969), 10.
[21]Augustine, *The Trinity* 1.1.3, *The Works of Saint Augustine: A Translation for the 21st Century*, vol. 1.5, trans. Edmund Hill (Brooklyn, NY: New City Press, 1991), 67.

practice theology for the sake of others, our task is to make the claims of the faith as understandable as possible so that other people can see how their lives relate to it. We do this even when, and perhaps especially when, the recipients of our teaching do not see the need for it.

In light of the challenges that come along with this task, we can point to four specific ways that theologians can build up the church through their theological work. These suggestions are by no means exhaustive, but taken together, they provide a framework from which we can begin to think about how a theologian can contribute to the ministry and mission of the church.

The first way is the most central: we build up the church by helping the church's members interpret Scripture better. Our own insights cannot be the focus of our instruction; rather, our primary purpose is to help the church understand the Bible. We give doctrinal instruction, Calvin says, in order to "open a way for all children of God into a good and right understanding of Holy Scripture."[22] This does not mean that theology is nothing more than biblical exegesis, although it cannot be less than that. Faithful theological instruction adheres to the biblical text and explains what it says, but it also goes beyond the text by drawing out its implications. We practice theology by starting with this question: In light of everything the Bible tells us, what also must be true about God, reality and history and the church's participation in it? Then, we seek to answer this question for the benefit of the church. Answering this question both faithfully and relevantly requires that we stay attuned to the content of Scripture, on the one hand, and to the concrete situation of the church and the world, on the other.

This insight leads to the second point: we build up the church by practicing theology from within the church. We will not be able to instruct the church faithfully if we remain isolated from the church's daily life and practices. Theologians cannot merely be a part of the church; they must be invested in the church. Because we exist in Christ and the Spirit—and

---

[22]John Calvin, "Subject Matter of the Present Work: Preface to the French Edition of 1560," in *Institutes of the Christian Religion*, Library of Christian Classics 20, trans. Ford Lewis Battles, ed. John T. McNeill (Philadelphia: Westminster Press, 1960), 7.

the church is the body of Christ and the temple of the Spirit—the church's life is intrinsically connected to our life, and we have to love it as we do ourselves. We express this love to the church's members by seeking to know them. This means hearing their questions, feeling the weight of the challenges they face and assessing how they are thinking, speaking and living in relation to God. Then, based on what we hear and see, we offer instruction. Often, this takes the form of encouragement, but sometimes it takes the form of criticism of the church's speech and actions. As theologians, we must have the courage to correct the church in light of what God has revealed. For example, we might ask the church whether it has been negatively influenced by outside sources, such as by the presuppositions that govern the wider culture's view of the way things are. We then may challenge these assumptions in light of Scripture's account of God's plan and call the church to change its views. We issue this call, however, not with a posture of superiority but in humility and with the goal of strengthening the church by better equipping it to live faithfully with God and think rightly about God.

Third, we build up the church when we help it think and live creatively. While much of our work as theologians involves pulling the church back to earlier formulations in order to help its thought and speech better correspond to Scripture, sometimes we have to push the church to think and speak in new and different ways so that it can deliver the gospel message faithfully. After all, the meaning of our words differs from culture to culture, and language itself changes over time. And, as Kevin Vanhoozer notes, the "truth of Jesus Christ is not supra- but transcultural. If it is universal, this not because it is suspended in some cultureless realm but precisely because it is able to descend into a myriad of cultures."[23] The reality that the gospel can enter into different cultural idioms and forms means that our knowledge of God must be communicated in distinct ways in different times and places. The existence of this diversity is not something to be feared or overcome but something to be embraced as a work of God.

---

[23]Kevin Vanhoozer, *The Drama of Doctrine* (Louisville, KY: Westminster John Knox, 2005), 323.

Theologians lead the way in helping the church figure out how to offer this embrace. Sometimes our task is to question whether ways of speaking that were faithful in the past remain so today. It may be the case that speaking God's truth in the present requires us to say something new and different than before. Calvin makes this point when he says that "we ought to seek from Scripture a sure rule for both thinking and speaking to which both the thoughts of our minds and the words of our mouths should be conformed. But what prevents us from explaining in clearer words those matters in Scripture which perplex and hinder our understanding, yet which conscientiously and faithfully serve the truth of Scripture itself, and are made use of sparingly and modestly and on due occasion?"[24] In this light, one of our key tasks as theologians is to spur efforts of theological translation within the church. For example, we might help the church figure out how to explain the content of biblical concepts and classical doctrines in new ways in order to express their meaning more accurately for a particular time or culture. We do so not to depart from past teaching, or merely in order to be creative and innovative, but to adhere more closely to what God has revealed. The Spirit guides us in this process by helping us understand the content of God's revelation in the past and recognize how God intends this revelation to shape the church in the present.[25]

The need for the Spirit's ongoing guidance reflects the reality that our knowledge of God involves more than facts or concepts but "itself is an act, an active participation in the process of knowledge which comes from God and returns to him."[26] This way of proceeding presupposes that God is a living God, and as such, he continues to work in new and surprising ways. To know him rightly, we have to keep up with what he is

---

[24]Calvin, *Institutes of the Christian Religion*, 1.13.3.

[25]See the point of J. Todd Billings: "Since the Spirit enables different receptions of Scripture to lead to the knowledge of Jesus Christ, we should be attentive to the Spirit's work by learning from culturally diverse receptions of Scripture. Culturally informed differences in Scripture interpretation . . . are not simply a problem to be overcome; they are a sign of the Spirit's work in indigenizing the gospel, that is, something to be celebrated!" See *The Word of God for the People of God: An Entryway into the Theological Interpretation of Scripture* (Grand Rapids: Eerdmans, 2010), 117.

[26]Karl Barth, *Church Dogmatics* III/2 (Edinburgh: T&T Clark, 1960), 179.

doing in the world, especially when this action takes place in times, places and cultures different from our own.

Fourth, and finally, we build up the church by participating in its mission. Christ lived and died in the world for the sake of the world, and the community that lives with him, shares his knowledge and exists as his body must do the same: it must exist *for* the world by living *in* the world and proclaiming Christ *to* the world. The church accomplishes this mission through the power of the Spirit who equips it for this task. "You will receive power when the Holy Spirit has come upon you," Jesus says, "and you will be my witnesses in Jerusalem, in all Judea and Samaria, and to the ends of the earth" (Acts 1:8). The primary form of this witness is the proclamation of the gospel, which comes to the world both as a word of hope and a call to repentance. As Paul preached to the Athenians, God commands "all people everywhere to repent, because he has fixed a day on which he will have the world judged in righteousness by a man whom he has appointed, and of this he has given assurance to all by raising him from the dead" (Acts 17:30-31).

The church proclaims this gospel message not as if we are throwing a stone but as an act of loving service. As Dietrich Bonhoeffer puts it, "the church is not there in order to fight with the world for a piece of its territory, but precisely to testify to the world that it is still the world, namely, the world that is loved and reconciled by God. . . . The church can only defend its own space by fighting, not for space, but for the salvation of the world."[27] Theologians provide leadership in equipping the church to proclaim the gospel accurately and in love. We do so by helping the church understand the content of the gospel more clearly and by holding its preaching and teaching accountable to Scripture. Beyond that, we serve the church's mission when our theological work bears faithful witness to Christ and to God's eternal plan through him.

Among other ways, our work bears witness to God when it engages the world on its own terms, as it really exists. This sometimes means using our theology to address the reality of suffering, both the spiritual

---

[27]Dietrich Bonhoeffer, *Ethics*, Dietrich Bonhoeffer Works, vol. 6, ed. Clifford Green (Minneapolis: Fortress, 2005), 63-64.

suffering that comes from sin and the physical suffering that stems from injustice. The challenge is that confronting either form of suffering will inevitably lead us into conflict with the powers and principalities as well as the rulers of the age. This is one of the ways that our thinking after Christ must be shaped by our life of obedience to Christ. Just as Christ's ministry always existed in tension with the rulers of his time, both religious and political, so must our ministry as theologians. To speak and think faithfully about Christ requires us, at certain points, to stand in conflict not only with the powers of our day but also with the tangible consequences of their work. We cannot be afraid when this happens. The earliest Christians recognized that to confess faith in Christ, and to obey him as Lord, means living as "aliens and exiles" in society (1 Pet 2:11). Living in such tension is not the goal of our relationship with Christ but its manifestation, and one of the ways we bear witness to Christ. "If any of you suffers as a Christian," Peter says, "do not consider it a disgrace, but glorify God because you bear this name" (1 Pet 4:16). Theologians do this by bringing the truth about God into the world through our work, and doing so—along with the rest of the church—out of love and for the sake of its salvation even when it comes at great cost.

6. We practice theology as disciples when we pursue both truth and unity.

In his prayer in Gethsemane, Jesus linked the church's mission to the unity of its members with God and one another. "I ask not only on behalf of these, but also on behalf of those who will believe in me through their word, that they may all be one. As you, Father, are in me and I am in you, may they also be in us, so that the world may believe that you have sent me" (Jn 17:20-21). This unity happens not because the distinction between the church's members has been erased but because each member is drawn together into God's triune life through the missions of the Son and the Spirit. "For just as the body is one and has many members, and all the members of the body, though many, are one body, so it is with Christ. For in the one Spirit we were all baptized into one body—Jews or Greeks, slaves or free—and we were all made to drink of one Spirit" (1 Cor 12:12-13). Our unity with one another in Christ and the Spirit counteracts the effects of sin, which always produces broken relationships. From the story of Adam and Eve in the garden to the murder of Abel by Cain to the dispersal of the nations in the tower of Babel, the story of humanity has been disunity. The church bears witness to God's overcoming of sin in the very fact that it contains people from "every tribe and language and people and nation" (Rev 5:9). Peoples formerly divided are "brought near by the blood of Christ" to form a "new humanity" (Eph 2:13-15). In line with this saving work, Paul argues that "a life worthy of the calling" found in the gospel is one that makes "every effort to maintain the unity of the Spirit in the bond of peace. There is one body and one Spirit, just as you were called to the one hope of your calling, one Lord, one faith, one baptism, one God and Father of all, who is above all and through all and in all" (Eph 4:1-6).

However, this call to unity poses a challenge for theologians: how can theologians build up the church as one unified body when there are so many disagreements within it regarding the truth of God? Ephraim Radner addresses this question by arguing that it begins from a false dichotomy. The assumption that unity and truth can be placed in competition with one another—as if we could have unity only if we abandon truth, or have truth if we break away from unity—wrongly defines these terms in light of the fallen realities of human life rather than according to God's eternal being.[28] We have to begin instead with the fact that the church exists by participation in Christ and the Spirit, who themselves are one with the Father. In the triune life, unity and truth are not in competition with one another but exist perfectly together, and this unity and truth are reflected in the gifts God gives to the church. As Radner notes, we "do not tend to see gentleness and patience as ever being in tension; we do not ever place kindness and self-control over and against each other. . . . Paul does not do this, presumably, because the fruit of the Spirit belongs to a singular existence that has been joined, as one, to the crucified life of Christ Jesus in its coherence, a life incapable of being

---

[28]Ephraim Radner, *Hope Among the Fragments: The Broken Church and Its Engagement with Scripture* (Grand Rapids: Brazos Press, 2004), 112.

parceled out in distinctive elements."[29] The same principle holds for
God's truth and unity: both qualities define the reality into which the
church is called to live.

This insight helps us see how we must proceed in our theological work
in the midst of a divided church. As theologians, we must seek the unity
of the church without presupposing that this unity means that we have to
compromise our commitment to truth; and we seek God's truth without
assuming that this will inevitably lead us to turn away from a commitment
to unity. Adopting this mindset requires that we view our theological opponents as members of our own family. We became family when we were
"baptized into Christ" (Gal 3:27), and we live together because Christ
shares his table with us (1 Cor 10:16). In our personal lives, we do not immediately cast our family members away when disagreements arise, but
we seek to reconcile with them. The same should be true for the children
of God. Our first act when we encounter a fellow Christian in error is to
check our own "selfish ambition" and put the other's interests before our
own (Phil 2:2-4). Then, when we know that we are acting for their sake,
we seek to lead them into the truth by turning to Scripture and asking the
Spirit for guidance. We approach them gently and repeatedly (Gal 6:1),
and only after multiple attempts to reconcile do we break away from them
(Rom 16:17; Tit 3:10-11). When and if we break from them, we do not use
this moment to vindicate ourselves or declare ourselves superior. Rather,
we take the opportunity to show them mercy and love.

Once again, Christ serves as our example.[30] At the Last Supper, Jesus
dined with Judas even though he knew that Judas was under the power
of the devil (Jn 13:2). And as Judas was about to betray him, Jesus still
washed his feet along with those of the rest of the disciples. Christ showed
mercy and love to Judas until the end, even as Judas turned away from
him and Jesus told him to do what he must do (Jn 13:27). This is what it
looks like to embody God's truth and unity at the same time. They exist
together when we humbly unite ourselves to others in self-sacrificial,
self-giving love even as they turn from the truth and go their own way.

[29]Ibid., 112-13.
[30]For this reading, see Radner, Hope Among the Fragments, 116.

7. We practice theology as disciples when we display confidence while avoiding defensiveness.

We know God faithfully when, among other things, we are not ashamed of the gospel (Rom 1:16). Our lack of shame is a matter of intellectual integrity. If we confess that Jesus is Lord and believe that God raised him from the dead, then we should be able to tell others about Jesus with confidence. The fact that our confidence flows from our faith in Christ means, however, that we express it within the context of a life whose predominant theme is humility.

This confident yet humble posture has its basis in our unique starting point. To practice theology in faith is to presuppose from the outset that the claims of our faith are true even if we do not immediately understand precisely *how* they are true. Due to our lack of understanding, we are called to "grow in the grace and knowledge of our Lord and Savior Jesus Christ" (2 Pet 3:18). We do so not in order to verify our claims after the fact but in order to grasp them more fully. We are confident because we are certain that God really has come to us in Christ and the Spirit. We know that if we trace out what must be true in light of who Christ is and what he has done through the help of his Spirit, then our thoughts will correspond to the truth of God. This takes a burden off our shoulders, because our confidence rests in God's action rather than our own. We are not called to have perfect theology; we are called to order our thinking around Jesus as best we can. In line with this, while James makes it clear that teachers will be held to a higher standard and "judged with greater strictness," he also makes it clear no one is perfect: "for all of us make many mistakes" (Jas 3:1-2). We will not be measured by the perfection of our knowledge but by whether or not we have been faithful to bring our knowledge in alignment with Jesus as he has been revealed to us.

We put this kind of faithfulness on display when we are willing to learn from others, change our minds and repent of a mistake. These tend to be rare traits among theologians, especially in the modern period. Among the negative side effects of pursuing theology within a university is the fact that theologians have approached their work as if their goal were to create a system of knowledge that is defensible against any form of critique or question. This system then functions as a framework through which every question and idea is filtered and then answered. In this approach, the traits of being open to mystery and willing to change one's views are seen as vices rather than virtues. After all, a willingness to retract a claim or change one's views betrays weakness before others, or perhaps even a lack of intellectual skill or confidence.

But theologians who proceed in faith should expect to be constantly changing and refining their views. This follows not only from the reality that God's divine being is incomprehensible to us but also from the fact that we know God by grace through faith. The act of changing our views is not a sign of weakness but of humility. "God's truth," Calvin says, "requires the kind of knowledge that will strip us of all confidence in our ability, deprive us of all occasion for boasting, and lead to submission."[31] We are not submissive in the sense that we hold our convictions softly or with a sense of embarrassment. We must be willing to defend the truth of God and the gospel of Christ. But we cannot be defensive about our personal views or our standing before others. We pursue theology faithfully when we believe it would be far better for us to be proven wrong about a theological issue—and for the truth about God to be proclaimed as a result—than for us to win an argument and the falsehood remain. Our desire to know Christ must be greater than our desire to be right, comfortable and secure in our ideas. The moment we stop revising our claims about God is the moment that we have ceased to be shaped by the reality that our knowledge comes as a gift of God and that he has given us this gift so that we might serve him.

Hebrews warns us to be careful that "none of you may be hardened by the deceitfulness of sin" (Heb 3:13). We express this care, and practice theology faithfully, when we embrace the chance to have our views challenged by others, especially those with whom we disagree. We cannot see our critics as our enemies or play the victim as if any opposition to us is by nature mean-spirited, unfair or ungenerous. Rather, we have to view our critics as our friends, as gifts from God that God uses to refine our

[31]Calvin, *Institutes of the Christian Religion*, 2.1.2.

knowledge and perhaps lead us to repent from mistakes. We cannot act like partisans for our particular point of view, called to defend it at all costs for the sake of our particular party. We must act like sinners who have been joined to Christ and who are following after him in faith and obedience. Among other things, following Christ means "becoming like him in his death" (Phil 3:10), and one of the ways we do this is by being willing to lose our standing before others if it means that Christ is proclaimed truly.

Paul reflects this mindset when he offers instructions to Timothy about matters of doctrine. He begins by telling Timothy to "fight the good fight of the faith; take hold of the eternal life, to which you were called and for which you made the good confession in the presence of many witnesses" (1 Tim 6:12). His point is that Timothy should defend the faith on the ground of the gospel of Christ and no other. His defense is not to be a *self*-defense—as if it were about Timothy—but rather a defense grounded in the promises made by Jesus. In line with this, Paul tells him: "I know the one in whom I have put my trust, and I am sure that he is able to guard until that day what I have entrusted to him. Hold to the standard of sound teaching that you have heard from me, in the faith and love that are in Christ Jesus. Guard the good treasure entrusted to you, with the help of the Holy Spirit living in us" (2 Tim 1:12-14). Note how Paul links his own trust in Christ to the fact that Christ himself will prove true in the end. Paul does not base his confidence in himself or his own views but on his trust in the judgment of the living Christ and the help of the Spirit. He makes a similar point a few chapters later: "in the presence of God and of Christ Jesus, who is to judge the living and the dead, and in view of his appearing and his kingdom, I solely urge you: proclaim the message; be persistent whether the time is favorable or unfavorable; convince, rebuke, and encourage, with the utmost patience in teaching" (2 Tim 4:1-2). Again, Paul locates the confidence Timothy should have in his teaching and preaching directly in Christ and the reality that Christ himself will judge the message Timothy proclaims.

This advice applies to all theologians: Christ is the source of our confidence because our ability to know God rests solely in him. We proceed as theologians knowing that he will prove true in the end, even if he does so against our own theological statements and belief. In light of this reality, we cannot be defensive about our ability to hold this knowledge rightly, because we know that we are faulty and may sometimes need to repent and change. We simply seek to be faithful to him by bearing witness to him, and doing so with confidence that, as the living Lord, he himself will confirm or correct our claims in time.

8. We practice theology as disciples by utilizing the insights of non-theological disciplines to enrich our thinking.

Theology operates differently than every other academic discipline. As we have seen, the difference is not that theologians operate by faith while other scholars operate by reason; rather, theologians begin with a distinct set of assumptions about the content of reason and how we relate to it. We presuppose that true reason is identical to God's eternal wisdom, which consists of his perfect knowledge of himself and all things. From this starting point, we confess that God's wisdom can be known only by God's grace, which comes to us when Jesus Christ gives us a share in his mind through his Spirit. Other disciplines begin in a different place. They presuppose, for example, that claims can be counted as rational and true when they can be confirmed by direct observation or on the basis of claims that stand in line with such observation. The difference between these two approaches runs parallel to Paul's distinction between "God's wisdom" and the "wisdom of this age" (1 Cor 2:6-7).

The existence of such differences does not mean that insights drawn from other disciplines cannot make contributions to our theological work. In fact, theologians have always assumed that thinkers from other disciplines make true claims on the basis of their unique disciplinary starting points. For example, Augustine argues that "all true and good Christians should understand that truth, wherever they may find it, belongs to their Lord."[32] Even the pagans, he says, offer true claims that theologians can and should embrace in their theological work. That they can do so stems from the reality that the God we know by faith is the

---

[32]Augustine, *On Christian Doctrine* 2.18.28.

same God who orders the natural world according to his will. The psalmist reflects this when he says that "the heavens are telling the glory of God, and the firmament proclaims his handiwork" (Ps 19:1). Paul echoes the same point by arguing that God's "eternal power and divine nature, invisible though they are, have been understood and seen through the things he has made" (Rom 1:20). He also notes that the human conscience "bears witness" to God's law to the extent that even Gentiles "do instinctively what the law requires" (Rom 2:14-15). On the basis of such claims, it is right to conclude that careful study of the natural order or the human mind—such as the kind of study performed by scientists, psychologists and sociologists—can lead them to make claims that correspond to the truth that God has revealed about these things in and through his saving work. Such claims can enrich our understanding of God's creation. A scientist, for example, might be able to tell us something true about creation that can give us new insights into the created order and our place within it; a psychologist may be able to reveal truths about the human mind that help us grasp the nature of our human condition more clearly; and a sociologist might help us understand how human communities function in a way that enriches our understanding of both the church and society.

At this point, however, a qualification must be issued, because if we are to say that "all truth is God's truth wherever it may be found," we have to define carefully what we mean by this phrase. We do not mean that everything we initially judge to be true, in fact, corresponds directly to the truth of God.[33] Interpreting the statement this way would make our own limited and potentially faulty judgment the arbiter of what counts as true. But it is quite possible that, due to our finite limitations and the effects of sin, our judgments can be mistaken. We might encounter true claims but not recognize them as true, believe that true claims are false and false claims are true, and be unable to understand how true claims are, in fact, true. In any of these cases, combining our faulty judgments with the revealed truth of God will inevitably distort our understanding

---

[33]For a development of this point, see Arthur Holmes, *All Truth Is God's Truth* (Grand Rapids: Eerdmans, 1977), 8-9.

of what God has revealed by shaping it according to our misperceptions. To avoid this error, when we say "all truth is God's truth wherever it may be found," we should mean that any truth we allegedly discern must correspond to God's eternal wisdom in order to be counted as true. And we should acknowledge that, while we can know the content of God's wisdom in the present, we do so only by faith as a result of God's revelation to us in Christ and the Spirit. This means that our knowledge of God's wisdom in the present is true but provisional. Only God himself has a complete understanding of how all the truths that can be discerned by reflecting upon the created order stand in continuity with the content of his divine wisdom. Until we see things as he does, we can count external truths as standing in continuity with God's truth—and thus utilize them in our theological work—only when they correspond to what we know of God through our faith in Christ by the Spirit.

On the basis of this distinction, we can draw two conclusions about how we should engage the insights of other academic disciplines in our work as theologians. First, we can and should seek out and embrace the insights of other disciplines. The fact that scholars studying non-theological disciplines can make true claims as a result of their rational reflections on the created order means we cannot withdraw from the rest of the scholarly world and fail to engage with what they have to say. "In Christ," Bonhoeffer says, "we are invited to participate in the reality of God and the reality of the world at the same time, the one not without the other."[34] The notion that we could do theological work while shuttered off from the world is a "counsel of despair," he argues, "a sacrifice made only at the cost of intellectual integrity."[35] As Karl Barth argues, we would be "foolish and ungrateful" if we ignored truth claims from the natural order, because God might be giving them to us precisely in order to help us "illuminate, accentuate or explain the biblical witness" more clearly.[36] Augustine's analogy of the ancient Israelites who took the Egyptians' golden idols with them as

[34]Dietrich Bonhoeffer, *Ethics*, Dietrich Bonhoeffer Works, vol. 6, ed. Clifford Green (Minneapolis: Fortress, 2005), 55.
[35]Dietrich Bonhoeffer, *Letters and Papers from Prison*, Dietrich Bonhoeffer Works, vol. 8, ed. John W. De Gruchy (Minneapolis: Fortress, 2009), 478.
[36]Karl Barth, *Church Dogmatics* IV/3.1 (Edinburgh: T&T Clark, 1961), 115-16.

they escaped from slavery is helpful here. They took the idols not in order to worship these idols but to reforge them and use them in a manner worthy of God. In the same way, we can take insights originally derived by non-Christians and elevate them by using them to say true things better than we could otherwise.[37] To refuse to use these insights would be to deny God's provision, to turn away from the very resources God has provided to us to sustain and enrich our theological work.

This insight leads to the second conclusion, which we must hold together with the first: we have to measure every truth claim we encounter by the criterion of God's revelation in Jesus Christ as recorded in Scripture. If truth claims derived from scholarly reflection on God's created order reflect the truth of God, they will correspond to what God reveals about these things in Scripture, where his truth is "more intimately and also more vividly" revealed.[38] So, we must take every truth claim we receive from another discipline and measure it by what Scripture says to see how it corresponds. This process of testing has the potential to enrich our theological work and, through us, the life of the church as a whole. Specifically, because the truth claims arising from reflection on the created order have to be measured by Scripture in order to be confirmed as true, we have to turn again and again to the Bible in order to figure out whether or not the claims we are receiving from other disciplines are, in fact, correct. This task enriches us by giving us better discernment about not only the content of other disciplines but also of Scripture itself. While truths derived from the created order will not contradict Scripture, the process of recognizing and testing them can prompt us to read Scripture with new eyes. God often works to renew his church in this precise way. By prompting us to ask new questions and develop new insights as a result of our engagement with people outside the church, God spurs us to reformulate past interpretations and develop new ones based on a fresh reading of Scripture. Our engagement with these external insights thus makes us better theologians and becomes the means by which God shapes his church by prompting us to acquire a better understanding of Scripture.

---

[37] Augustine, *On Christian Doctrine* 2.40.60.
[38] Calvin, *Institutes of the Christian Religion*, 1.10.1.

Together, these two conclusions mean that as theologians, we should approach other academic disciplines with openness rather than hostility. We engage ideas from other sources knowing that the created order exists within the context of God's providential plan for history. We know that we cannot uncritically accept every truth claim we receive from other disciplines, because all truth corresponds to God's truth, not the other way around. Yet the fact that we test and measure their claims does not diminish but elevates these disciplines, because it allows their naturally derived yet true insights to be appropriated into the biblical framework. In this way, the truths of academic learning are perfected as they are adapted and adopted into the true history, meaning and purpose of the world—the very history, meaning and purpose that the church bears witness to through its life, proclamation and ministry. This is how the created order can be said to declare "the glory of God" and "proclaim his handiwork" (Ps 19:1). It does so because, by placing this order within the context of God's eternal plan for history, its truths can serve and enrich the ministry of the Word, which is the proclamation of God's plan for the world in Jesus Christ. He is the key to seeing and interpreting all reality and history because everything in creation—including the other academic disciplines and the scholars who operate within them—has been made through him and for him in the context of God's plan to unite all things in him (Jn 1:3; Eph 1:10).

9. We practice theology as disciples when we pursue our theological work with joy.

Paul's command that we should "rejoice in the Lord always" directs our practice of theology (Phil 4:4). Our joy begins where our new life begins: with Christ's redemption of us from our sin so that we can live as God's children and share in his love through the power of his Spirit. We have joy because we know that when we pursue theological work, we do so as partners of Christ and all those who also have been joined to him by the Spirit. We have been made participants in the long history of their work and have been given the opportunity to add our contribution it. We rejoice because this means that our lives as theologians are not aimless but purposeful. We have been tasked with the mission of testifying to God's grace so that others may know and live in it as well.

The fact that we can contribute to God's eternal plan in this way does not make us self-satisfied, because our work is not about building ourselves up or serving our own advantage. Rather, our work is an act of worship, one that anticipates the worship we will offer God into eternity. We find joy because God uses our work to enrich the church so that people might know him better. We are joyful when God uses our work to lead others to a deeper communion with him by helping them live in closer alignment with his will and plan. We reflect this joy in the way that we approach others, not as fault-finders seeking to correct them but as fellow pilgrims seeking to obey God together with them. We reflect it when we seek intellectual and moral purity precisely so we can be prepared to bear witness to Christ more faithfully. We find God's joy when we immerse ourselves in the words of Scripture, paying attention to every detail, so that we might see more clearly how God has brought all the small moments of history together to form a single story of salvation for our sake and the sake of the world.

At their best, the builders of great cathedrals took great joy in placing every stone and pane of glass in its right place. They did this work not for their own benefit or simply in order to create a magnificent building. They did it for God, because one of the ways a Christian worships a God who has worked through the small things—things like a bush, a slingshot and a manger—is to use the small things to worship him. The best theologians stand in this same tradition. By examining every word and idea critically, and by figuring out how to use these words to think and speak about God rightly, we honor the God who has worked through words to order history for our salvation. Every word matters, no matter how small, because the whole creation is ordered to bear testimony to God and his love. So, our work goes on as we pick up the pieces by finding one more word or idea to take captive to Christ. There is joy in the process, because we know that the God to whom our words are directed is a God who will receive them, despite all our faults, as an offering that fills him with joy.

SUBJECT INDEX

SCRIPTURE INDEX

Finding the Textbook You Need

The IVP Academic Textbook Selector
is an online tool for instantly finding the IVP books
suitable for over 250 courses across 24 disciplines.

www.ivpress.com/academic/